FIRED UP for Life!

How To Get & Stay Motivated

GREG A. GERRIE

First Edition – July 2013

ISBN
978-1-4602-1872-3 (Hardcover)
978-1-4602-1873-0 (Paperback)
978-1-4602-1874-7 (eBook)

Editorial Team
S. Cummings, G. Gerrie

Produced by:

FriesenPress
Suite 300 – 852 Fort Street
Victoria, BC, Canada V8W 1H8

www.friesenpress.com

Distributed to the trade by The Ingram Book Company

Contents

PROMISES

The verbs used in the following statements include *give, show, teach, share, sell, demonstrate and persuade.* The underlying implication is that it is *you* who must decide, *you* who must do the work and *you* who must commit. And, when you do, the promises are very real.You *can* and *will* accomplish these wonderful objectives. Believe me, if I can do it so can you. Here are those objectives:

1. Give you the kind of hope and encouragement that will help you to live life with joy.
2. Show you a way to leave behind pain and regret and replace it with peace.
3. Teach you *the* most important aspect of living which is seeking wisdom and truth.
4. Share with you how to go after the right kind of success – success that brings lasting joy.
5. Sell you on the fact that you are not stuck with your past, that you can develop new beliefs and attitudes to transform your life positively and forever.
6. Demonstrate the power of turning failures into successes.
7. Help you develop an exciting new vision for all areas of your life and show you how to *dream the possible dream*.
8. Show you how to live well and finish beautifully.
9. Teach you how to think and speak with power, passion and purpose and how that will change *your* mind and the mind of others.

10. Encourage you to foster high quality relationships that will enrich the lives of others as well as yours.

11. Persuade you to take care of your billion dollar body.

12. Help you to maximize your days so you can have the *time of your life*.

13. Remind you to surround yourself with people and environments that will propel you toward your goals.

14. Have you realize that the greatest gift of success to yourself will occur when you give the gift of yourself to others.

15. Help you see that you are a unique individual, that you've been a winner from the start and that you have a very special purpose.

It's never too late to be the person you should have been.

MAJOR DALE COLLIE-US RANGERS (RETIRED)

FOREWORD

By Dr. Peter Legge
President-Canada Wide Magazine,
Speaking Professional, CSP, CPAE

If you buy only one book this year, it should be this wonderful motivation book by Greg Gerrie.

All of us have dreams, visions, and goals for our lives, careers, families, communities and nation.Very often we need to get motivated toward action; we need someone, something, or, in this case, a book. Greg Gerrie's first book will get you going, giving you practical insights by successfully blending the wisdom of the ages and scribes who have come before.This book will guide you along the mysterious path of motivation and take you through a carefully thought out route into the future. We don't have to start over . . . we can build upon the rich heritage that has been passed down to us from others.

Greg has done his research well, using practical knowledge from some of the greatest motivational achievers in our generation. He has also blended in his own experiences as a professional speaker and lecturer. He shares his own vision and demonstrates how vital motivation is to the accomplishment of our goals, just how important motivation is.

My friend and professional speaking colleague Greg Gerrie has discovered that life *does* work when it is lived from the inside out. He teaches that motivation must begin from within all of us and be expressed in our everyday actions.

This book is a winner . . . and so is Greg Gerrie.

THANK YOU

THANK YOU — THANK YOU!

As I went through the timeline of my life, the people I remembered the most were those who believed in me. They were the people who in a very special way saw things in me that I could not.

My thanks to Zig Ziglar, for being an author and speaker of integrity and who made one of the greatest contributions to my life by his unabashed profession of faith in the Lord. Dave Phillips, whose constant, unceasing support in my business and personal life has been a Godsend. Never have I met a man so dedicated and willing to help people, a man selfless in the service of others and to the betterment of mankind. His sense of humour, his warm compassion, his love, and his joy for living have motivated and inspired me more times than I can count. Dr. Peter Legge, professional speaker and busy CEO of Canada Wide Magazine for supporting and doing the foreword for my book. The Roberts, for warmly making me a part of their family. Jeff Gunther, the first to hand me the world's best selling book, and a close friend of the heart. Ruth & Stan Cummings, for their love, care, and support of my book and my life. My sisters Gale and Rhonda, for our exceptional relationship of unconditional love. My Dad, for his strength, his integrity, and his encouragement of this book and my life, and my Mom, for teaching me the positive characteristics of consideration, care, and love for others.

I would also like to thank Mrs. Gullickson, my very kind kindergarten teacher, Rex Glover my first all-star hockey coach, Wendell Greghan, my grade six teacher who helped me win my first public speaking contest, Victor Fleury, my grade seven teacher who role-modeled inspiration, Ms. Campbell, my high school science teacher who made me feel like I was important, Bill Oliver, for his friendship, Julie Ferguson of Beacon Literary Services (my book mentor), my students Carolina Kern, Soraiya Campbell, Vivian Yin and Alanna Linder for their passion for life and David Bentall, for his fantastic support and encouragement in some very tough times.

In the third edition of this book, a good friend Mary came out of nowhere to re-edit this work making it more credible. She is both a lover and servant of God whom I pray will be blessed mightily for her faith and positive mental "fired-up" attitude.

YOU

ARE WORTH IT

I wrote this book because I wanted to help you to be successful, to enjoy your life and to gain a deeper understanding of life's purpose for you. I wanted to share my mistakes, my victories and the wisdom I have gained thus far in life so that you might benefit. My hope is that the book helps you to reach your goals in a satisfying way that leads to lifelong success. I wanted to encourage you who may be down on life, whether broken in relationship, financially in trouble, deeply hurt over an incident, struggling with career, experiencing a health challenge, or seeking a deeper meaning. I want you to understand the awesome, the magnificent, and the unbelievable potential that is in everyone…including you!

I recognize that we must all make our own mistakes and that part of the meaning of life is to learn from those mistakes. But experiencing mistakes vicariously from a book is far different than actually making your own mistakes. In life we keep learning new lessons until we finally understand. My hope is that this book will help you understand some of the basic principles of success before you have to experience some painful lessons that are perhaps unnecessary and life-damaging. One of the tenets in this book is that you must boldly put new ideas into action. You must decide what you want and fearlessly go after it. Invariably, you will make mistakes, however, remember that roots grow deeper in trees exposed to fierce wind.

The most important message throughout this book is that no matter what your circumstances, it is the self-chosen beliefs and attitudes which will count most in helping you to discover new joy and success in the game of life.

This book will inspire you to go beyond what you thought was possible. Drink it all in and apply it now.

YOU are worth it - you REALLY are worth it!

PART I

Motivation and Success

1

BUILD YOUR CHARACTER — FORM THE FOUNDATION

Aaaaaaaahhhhhh yes, grade eight – I remember it all too well. I lived on a military base and went to a small middle school in Chatham, New Brunswick, Canada. Life was absolutely fantastic. I had two loving parents, two sisters to battle with, and a fine school with excellent teachers. I played A-level rep hockey for the local town of Chatham and was learning the game of golf in the summers. In my grade eight year, I played for the school volleyball, basketball and hockey teams. I was also President of the student council and loved all the benefits and privileges associated with that. Academically I received the top mark in English, and was elected valedictorian of my graduating class. I would say that most people would have identified me as successful.

Then my Dad was posted to the nation's capital, Ottawa, and I had a dramatic shift in environment and lifestyle. I was off to a glowing start in that I made the senior school hockey team while only in grade nine. Being fourteen and skating with 18 year olds was quite a privilege. I made the honour roll in grade nine but after that I discovered other seemingly important areas to focus on. I wanted to play on as many sports teams as I could, go out with girls, party as much as possible, and above all, be cool. Throughout my time in the nation's capital, I played high calibre hockey for both the high school and Triple A all-star teams right up to midget (grade 12). As captain of my Midget A team, I played first line. Our high school team even took a trip to Sweden to play. What an awesome adventure! I also played for the school golf team. In short, I was having the time of my life. My sporting exploits provided opportunities to look good, to be cool and to be popular.

You will notice that there was little mention of my academic exploits after grade nine. My parents began to express concern about my drop in marks but being the smooth talking character that I was, I would always assure them that I was leading a "balanced" lifestyle. You see, one of my greatest strengths had always been communication. My parents had exposed me to the adult world very early in life and I developed an ability in communicating well with all adults, including my parents. This attribute also became my downfall because I believed that with communication I could talk my way in and out of anything. I could find the easy way out and where there was a shortcut I would find it. Talk was cheap; I could fool everyone but little did I know I was only fooling myself.

In my final year of high school my Dad was posted again and we moved to a smaller town in Ontario called Trenton. There, I experienced one of the most miserable years of my life. The smaller school was very cliquish and I stayed clear except to attend classes. I didn't even go to my own graduation ceremony. I made the Junior B hockey team in Belleville and spent a great deal of time on a bus or on the ice. By Christmas I was failing calculus and algebra and was running an average below sixty percent. If I was going to go to university, something had to be done.

After Christmas I decided to quit junior hockey to focus more on school. I also met with the school counsellor regarding what I should take in university. After an intensive investigation of my personality and attributes (eight minutes) he said that engineering would be best for me. So engineering it was. I buckled down and my average climbed sufficiently to be accepted into Carleton University in Ottawa.

University was yet another cornucopia of sport and party opportunities. While I did spend many hours working hard and studying, I also spent too many other hours being part of the statistic that had this university set pub records for the most beer consumed per capita of all Canadian universities. You see, I simply had not developed the most important aspect of living that one needs to survive and thrive in this society – *Discipline* was not an important word in my vocabulary. I later learned that discipline was not something you could turn on and off. It had to be developed as part of one's character. This takes time. It takes time to develop poor character traits and it takes time to develop good ones as well. After two year in engineering, my marks were not sufficient to continue.

My self-esteem was at its lowest point ever. The golden boy from grade eight who seemingly had a very bright future had fast-tracked himself to failure. I headed west in search of work and a new perspective on life. My goal was to land a position working as a labourer in construction. That was where the big money was. Regrettably, I arrived in Calgary to face a labour strike and was forced to look for work elsewhere. At five feet eight inches tall and one hundred and sixty-five pounds, I ended up working as a bouncer in a bar. (Now don't tell me God doesn't have a sense of humour!) There, I learned to see a different side of life. Perhaps it was the life where I was destined to end up in if I didn't shape up. I worked 7pm to 1am nightly and did everything from loading beer, to fending off intoxicated women, to breaking up bar room brawls involving overzealous cowboys who wouldn't remove their hats. We would also experience the joy of visitations from motorcycle gangs but they usually kept to themselves. (Praise God!) Each night, I would return to my apartment reeking from cigarettes and beer. Finally I landed a job in construction working 7am to 3pm. After work I would collapse in exhaustion for an hour, get up, grab some dinner and head for my night job as a bouncer. I was bringing in the bucks but burning myself out.

I extended my four-month break to a full year and eventually landed a position with an engineering firm. Here I succeeded wonderfully well and was sent to Ottawa, Vancouver and England as a technical representative. I thrived in the company because of my excellent communication skills and ability to work hard in an environment where I could see results. With renewed confidence I returned to Ottawa to complete my engineering program. After three months, it was apparent that I simply was not cut out for the academic world of engineering. My spirits had never been lower and I was somehow led to go see a counsellor. I poured my heart out to her explaining that I felt desperate, very lost and indeed, hopeless. This was my first real opportunity to hear a motivational speaker. This woman did something called a *re-frame*. "This is wonderful," she said. "It's the beginning of a whole new adventure for you. You have identified exactly what you're not good at. Now go find what you *are* good at." I will never forget her name, Dawn. Her viewpoint gave me a whole new reason to carry on. By the way, later on in life I took a personality profile called Birkman and there it identified Engineering as last in terms of what I was created for. I encourage people to take the time and money to understand what their gifts are. (see Dave Phillips at back of book for Birkman information.)

Once again I ended up working for another high-tech manufacturing firm and once again I thrived. I made significant contributions to the production process through some engineering innovations. I wrote a computer program, which automatically calculated some critical design specifications for electronic parts. The boss was impressed and so was I. But a new dream was looming on the horizon, a dream that had been lurking inside me for many years. I decided that I wanted to fly jets!

The Boyhood Dream

Only one in one thousand applicants receive their wings (pilot graduation) through the Canadian Armed Forces pilot training program. I submitted my application and was selected to go to Aircrew Selection in Toronto. Here I completed a multitude of medical, psychological, intelligence, and co-ordination tests over a number of days. I then returned to my hometown of Trenton, Ontario where each day I anxiously awaited the letter that would determine my future. Finally the letter arrived and with trembling hands I opened it. It read:

> **"Congratulations, you have been accepted into the Canadian Armed Forces pilot training program. You are to commence officer training on October 15, 1983."**

The excitement was overwhelming. I was "over the top" thrilled and had successfully completed the first leg of a wonderful dream.

There were four phases needed to complete training to become a military pilot. The first was basic officer training. This involved three months of intensive mental and physical training where discipline, leadership, enduring hardship, and soldiering were taught. I excelled in this phase of the training and seemed to be a natural leader within the platoon. The second phase was land and sea survival where post-crash survival and high altitude endurance were tested. Again, I passed this phase. Difficulty arose during the third phase called primary flying training. Much study was required in order to learn the basics of flight, air regulations, and meteorology. However, I pressed on and made it through phase three in Portage la Prairie, Manitoba. I remember how cold it was in Portage. I'm talking minus thirty degrees centigrade. Why, it was so cold that we used to see dogs frozen to the fire hydrants!

Finally, phase four had arrived. It was big time at the "Big 2." Moose Jaw, Saskatchewan is a town in the middle of the Canadian prairies with subzero winter temperatures and dry hot summers. It might be considered a less than desirable place for most people, but to Canadian pilots in training, it was heaven. Ground school required more intensive study including more meteorology, flight rules, emergency procedures, navigation, and aerodynamics. All day, we would hear the beautiful sound of jets taking off and landing while we studied week after week, month after month.

At last the day came when I would strap into the beautiful CT114 Tutor to take my first ride with an instructor. You may have seen the Canadian Snowbirds aerobatics team. The Tutor is the same aircraft used to train Canadian pilots. It is a two-seat single engine jet aircraft with a top speed 412 knots (470 mph or 750 km/h) and capable of handling a G-force of seven. (This is expressed as "you can pull 7 Gs"). We took off and reached the flying area and the instructor said "you have control" and control I took. I rolled the aircraft several times and did a few steep turns and climbs. What a remarkable flying machine. It was so fast, so responsive, a dream to fly. However, my desire to pull G's far exceeded my ability to withstand them. My confident voice turned to a whimpering plea to return to base as I swallowed hard to keep the contents of my stomach where they belonged.

[Note-A "G" represents the force of gravity. As you stand on earth, you are experiencing one G-force. When you go on rides at the fair and are being whipped around on a roller coaster, you might experience a two-G turn positively or a zero-G negative drop (weightless). Three Gs is when you have to start focusing on breathing management or you'll black out.]

Months of training passed and one day after being with my instructor and practising take-offs, landings, aerobatics and emergency procedures, we rolled up to the hanger. He flipped up his visor and looked over at me with serious eyes. His only words were, "It's time." I knew exactly what he meant. It was time to solo. I was thrilled! I was ecstatic ...I was positively scared!

Ecstasy

We walked back into the hanger and I signed out the aircraft in *my* name. I was responsible. This was *my* aircraft. It was *my* baby. It was a hot summer day with the heat waives emanating from the pavement. I walked back out onto the tarmac (runway where the aircraft is parked) and there I was – donned in a black flight suit, parachute, helmet and military flying sunglasses, walking toward my million-dollar aircraft... you know, kind of like actor Tom Cruise in the movie *Top Gun*. After starting up, taxiing out, and doing pre-flight checks, I spoke to the tower. "This is Bandit 711, ready for takeoff." The reply, "Bandit 711, you are cleared for takeoff." A final check on engine temperature and pressure, and I was rolling down the runway. I could feel the pressure of the acceleration as I sank in my seat-50, 60, 70 knots-rotate; I was off and flying. *Gear up, flaps up, temperature and pressure looking good*...In that moment a warm feeling of excitement filled my mind and body. My heart raced with joy. Soloing was oh so much sweeter than being with an instructor. I was experiencing the exhilaration of high flight and I now knew how WWII pilot John Magee felt.

High Flight

Oh I have slipped the surly bonds of earth,
And danced the skies on laughter-silvered wings.
Sunward I've climbed and joined the tumbling mirth
Of sun-split clouds and done a hundred things
You have not dreamed of-wheeled and soared and swung
High in the sun-lit silence,
Hov'ring there, I've chased the shouting wind along and flung
My eager craft through footless halls of air.
Up, up the long delirious, burning blue
I've topped the wind-swept heights with easy grace,
Where never lark, nor even eagle flew;
And while with silent, lifting mind I've trod,
The high untrespassed sanctity of space,
Put out my hand, and touched the face of God

—JOHN MAGEE, (MAGEE WAS AN AMERICAN PILOT IN THE RCAF DURING WW II WHO WAS SHOT DOWN THE DAY AFTER HE RECONCILED WITH GOD AND WROTE THIS POEM.)

After several take-offs and landings, I landed my aircraft and taxied to the hanger. With unabashed exuberance I could hardly contain myself. I had a grin so wide it made my face disappear. Off I went to the officer's club to celebrate. Oh sweet victory! It had taken me close to two years to get to this point and I was on the home stretch.

The final phase of training was called instrument flight rule (IFR) flying. This is taught so that when pilots fly in clouds or fog, they can navigate on target. It is also the main way that modern aircraft fly even in good weather. To learn IFR, you fly in good weather but a velcro-attached visor that angles downward at forty-five degrees is attached to your helmet. This ensures that you only see the instrument panel and are unable to look out the window. You fly by listening to tower instructions and watching the instruments that reveal where you are in the skies. As said, this is done to simulate flying in clouds or low visibility weather. On each successive IFR flight, the instructor would point out all the mistakes I was making, which is normal and natural but doubts began to creep in. Before each flight I would feel sick and visualise making mistakes. In my mind's eye I would see the instructor criticizing me for my mistakes and would become emotional. As a result, I started flying defensively, worrying more about making mistakes than concentrating on the task at hand. My focus was not on the joy of flying, but on the fear of failing. I also believed the instructors were too hard on me which I later learned was a defence mechanism. I was switched to another instructor, and then another. My self-esteem plummeted. I remember I use to argue and make excuses during debriefing. This is generally not a good idea. I was fighting to be acknowledged for what I *did* do well. Over the next three months, I fell further and further behind, so far in fact that I had to take the "do or die" test. I had to fly with the Chief Flying Instructor. My instructor told me to relax and not be afraid. He might as well have told me to stop breathing.

The test flight had gone well and the last procedure was a precision approach tower controlled instrument landing. All I had to do was ace this last part and I would be back on track. "Bandit 711, You're high on the glide-path - reduce your altitude," squawked the tower. I was in a daze. I was tense. I was nervous. I just wanted to get that aircraft on the ground. I followed the tower's instructions and corrected my flight attitude (angle of descent), but I forgot to trim the aircraft and so I ballooned back up. "You're high, you're high," tower said urgently. Once again I corrected. One more time, the controller gave me warning... and then it happened. The moment that every student pilot dreads arrived; the instructor ripped off the visor from my helmet. My heart sank into the depths of despair. What I should have seen out in front of me was a runway but instead, I saw prairie fields. The runway was far underneath me. I had overshot my landing point. "I have control," said the instructor in a calm voice. I pleaded with the instructor "Let me try it again. Please! I know I can do it!"

There was no response and he proceeded to land the aircraft. That would be the last time I would ever fly a Tutor. A review board met, and a week later I was sent packing. Feeling ashamed, downhearted, broken and depressed, I left the base without saying goodbye to the good friends I had made. I later applied to the United States, British and Australian air forces but it was no use. My dream was over. I felt devastated and empty inside. It would take me ten years to stop having bad dreams about flying.

It seemed that Greg Gerrie was learning many lessons at a young age. This is the kind of a story many of us have experienced in one way or another and you know, I'm glad it happened. The significant lesson in the story was that the failure was unnecessary. You see, it was not physical ability and co-ordination that was lacking in me, it was mental maturity - the powers of concentration, perseverance, discipline, and most importantly, the ability to believe in myself. It is a true story of how fear and self-sabotage impacted one man's dream. I share this experience as my signature story as I travel around speaking on success and failure. Every story has its lessons. The lessons and wisdom gained from this and other incidents in my life are what comprise the chapters that follow. In this chapter of my life, I had learned the following:

- **Setting goals in the high school years is crucial. Many fine young students are lost in school because they are given too much freedom to do whatever they want. Setting and achieving goals is a skill needed for one's entire life.**
- **Positive and negative habits and attitudes developed at a young age follow a person into their adult years. It is crucial to identify and correct poor habits and reinforce positive ones.**
- **We all have strengths and weaknesses. It is important to identify weaknesses in attitude and effort early. More importantly, we must focus on the development of the strengths.**
- **Identifying potential career paths through extensive testing and evaluation is an important part of the high school experience. Also, it is never too late to learn your strengths and gifts.**
- **Focusing on a dream, however large or small, with unrelenting conviction is essential to success.**
- **Learning to visualise a positive result brings success closer. Visualising a negative result manifests failure.**

- **Worry, fear, and anxiety are at the root of most failures and working to overcome this wrong way of thinking is absolutely critical to success.**

Chapter 1 — Summary

Build Your Character — Form a Foundation

- Set goals no matter how young or old you are.
- It takes time to develop a poor attitude but you *can* develop a good one in a short time with the right help.
- Focusing on a dream, however large or small, with unrelenting conviction is essential to success.
- Learning to visualise a positive result brings success closer. Visualising a negative result brings failure.
- Worry, fear, and anxiety are at the root of most failures.
- Sometimes you have to fail in order to learn what you don't know.

Stay Fired Up!

2

EXPERIENCE PAIN — GAIN WISDOM

I returned home to grieve my loss and to explore what I would do next. Luckily I had developed some strong relationships with some high-ranking people in the military and I was given a post at a military physical education centre in Trenton, Ontario. I will forever be grateful to General Garry King (deceased) and Major Bill Oliver (retired) for this time. It would be during this period that I would regain lost confidence.

I decided that a university degree was important if I was going to succeed in life. I was still only 25 years young and had my whole life ahead of me. By night, I continued to have nightmares about flying (not being able to get the aircraft on the ground) and by day I began to build a new life. Queen's University was just fifty miles down the road and I made an appointment with the Dean of Arts. I still remember the day I met with him. There he was, sitting behind his academic throne (big desk) with a plethora of degrees positioned all over the wall. I poured my heart out to him asking that I be accepted into the Faculty of Arts. He looked down his very long nose and replied, "Why don't you just stay in the military. It would appear you are more suited to that." Back then I didn't necessarily live by the Judeo Christian ethic. I immediately saw an image in my mind of a hand connected to *my* arm grabbing his nose and twisting it this way and that. But thankfully, this image was not manifested into action. After much pleading on my part he allowed me to take two courses on probation to see if I had what it took to attend the prestigious Queen's University.

On two nights each week for a year, I drove to Kingston taking an organisational development course and a writing course. I studied hard and earned a B in both courses. Not bad for a former academic failure. Furthermore I felt that I was making a meaningful contribution in my military position. As well, I was privileged to play on the team that won the Canadian Armed Forces (CAF) National Hockey Championships. In the summer of the same year, I won the CAF Ontario singles tennis championships and my Dad and I came second in doubles. To play with my Dad in a major championship was the opportunity of a lifetime. During this time period, I also passed my civilian private pilots licence and felt redeemed on a minor scale. It was quite a year and I *was* regaining my confidence.

The following year, I was then accepted into the Faculty of Arts to do a degree in Economics and a year later into the Faculty of Education to do a teaching degree. I became a respected member of the Queen's community by being a Don in residence and was on various faculty and residence committees. In fact, I ended up on a committee with the very person whose nose I wanted to twist. I don't think he recognized me, or at least he didn't acknowledge my presence. I attended Queen's for two and a half years solid without a break and earned a Bachelor of Arts in Economics and a Bachelor of Education. On graduation day, I was decked out in a suit and tie and the traditional Queen's robe and hood. My parents presented me with the finest gift I have ever received, a gold Queen's ring. It was a wonderful day and everyone involved was very proud. The ring symbolised that I *could* go from failure to success. I could win at life if I really wanted to. I did have "the right stuff."

From here I moved to Toronto to search for work. Although I was qualified as a teacher, for some reason I wanted to be in the fast paced world of business. While using the career centre facilities at the University of Toronto, the manager of the centre took notice of me and offered me a marketing position at the university. The pay and benefits were excellent so I took the position. In the same year, I had also landed a position as a tennis teaching professional at the luxurious Richmond Hill Country Club. My situation continued to progress.

The New Spiritual Search

At this point in my life I began searching for the spiritual meaning of my existence. Why are we here? What are we doing? What is the purpose of life? I was looking for answers. A friend told me about a communications program that had made a significant difference to her. She said it gave her an edge like nothing else. So I did what any success-seeking person would do, I enrolled in the program. It was the beginning of a new era in my life. At the end of the three days, I was very high, very excited and very motivated.

In the program, I saw the impossible become possible. I realized that we need to live our lives with vision, purpose, and values. I saw that so much more was possible by discovering the secrets of success and the power of wisdom. I wanted to learn as much as I could about human motivation. But sitting in a motivational seminar for three days is far different than *living* what was taught. I had more lessons to learn, painful lessons. It seemed that I was spending an inordinate amount of time at the seminar centre volunteering my services to help put more people into the courses. I later realized that the organisation had cult-like characteristics. It all seemed so progressive at the time.

I met a man in the program whom I was really excited about! You see, he was "successful." I mean he was married, drove a BMW, and was an eloquent talker. He was surely my ticket to becoming the success I dreamed about and so I placed my trust in him. I was so excited that he chose to make *me* his protégé. In order to make a long story short, our last conversation was left with him screaming at me because I wanted to get out of the business we were involved in together. I simply had not acquired the skills and discipline necessary to be an entrepreneur and I was losing a lot of money and following the wrong man with the wrong principles. This individual had also taken several of my friends for a ride to the tune of thousands of dollars, and their pension funds. I was to later learn that he ended up divorced. Apparently I had something to learn about whom to follow.

At the same time I had purchased a home with my sister. We bought it at the highest price on the market and later were to sell it at the lowest price. It was a financial disaster. After being rear-ended in my car three times in six months and then robbed at gun point by three masked men at a bank machine, I decided that I had had enough of Toronto. I could not get rid of the feeling that I needed to leave the city, so I packed up and headed west to Vancouver leaving my poor sister to manage the house.

Several months before my departure I had met a man named Jeff Gunther. He became a boarder at our home. He was a great guy, successful in business, and we became friends. The only strange thing about Jeff was that he would sit and read his Bible extensively. One Saturday night at about 2am, after I returned home from a night of carousing, he told me about Jesus Christ. I could not see how this Jesus could help me get rich so I forgot about the conversation. Later on, Jeff gave me a Bible. I tried reading it but it was full of gibberish and useless information. I did however read one of the chapters named Proverbs which had some good motivational and ethical advice.

When I arrived in Vancouver, I substitute taught at high schools and also taught tennis. At the same time, I began designing and developing success programs for teenagers. I wanted to teach them not to make the same mistakes that I had made. My seminars became popular and I went on to do programs for parents and then corporations. I was learning to powerfully communicate the importance of living life with vision and confidence. Meanwhile, I had accidentally left my Bible in Toronto. It arrived by mail shortly after my arrival with a note from Jeff:

> *Greg, no matter how many times you leave this Holy Bible behind I will always send it on after you. It is the single most important book you will ever read. It is the living Word of God, the instruction manual of life.* - Jeff

I thought that this was a bit fanatical but I liked Jeff and felt acknowledged by his perseverance.

A Key Turning Point

In 1992 I met a man named Dave Phillips. He too had a keen interest in helping youth and so we would meet regularly. Dave worked for Focus on the Family, a Christian organisation. While I *was* on a journey for spirituality, I really didn't have much time for that "religious stuff." I humoured Dave as he would try to introduce me to the so-called truth. Whatever we were talking about, invariably Dave would say, "You know, I just happened to have an audio-tape on that." Over the years I became educated about the validity of the Bible. I learned that religion was one thing, but a relationship with my Creator was quite another.

One day Dave had a spare ticket to Peter Lowe's Success 95 Conference. My mentor in the professional speaking community, world famous speaker and author Zig Ziglar, was going to be speaking. The speakers were awesome and leading up to the intermission the audience was warmly invited to hear about Zig and Peter's spiritual journey. Their testimony had no real impact on me but at the end of the conference, Zig's free tape was handed out. I listened to it all the way home. The message was so compelling, so powerful, and so truthful that I made Jesus Christ my Lord and Saviour that day. You have heard the term "born again." Well...I was! For those who do not understand the full story, the phrase "born again" can be perceived as fanatical based on the many zealous religious folks over the years who have tried to impart the word of God but have missed the mark replacing love with judgement and grace with rules. It had taken me five years of education and research to understand enough of the Bible and Jesus Christ to make a decision. (Beliefs can be hard to break.) It was not a decision made quickly or easily but...it was the best decision I have ever made. I have since learned that it will be the best decision I *ever* will make as well.

Note: The paragraph you have just read is the most important one in this book. There is a way to unquestionably prove beyond any shadow of a doubt that the Bible really is the *inspired* Word of God.

Becoming a Christian does not make one's life easier. In fact, in many ways it becomes harder. While you do have access to more peace, God does not come down and fix everything in your life...darn it. You still have to work, and all the principles of success apply. In fact, as I grew to know the Bible, I found that much of what the great speakers, philosophers, and my Dad were teaching exemplified core principles from the Good Book. Despite my new faith, another disaster was looming on the horizon.

Two years after finding my new faith, I met a Christian stockbroker. You may be thinking now there's an oxymoron if you ever heard one. We became good friends and I expressed to him my dissatisfaction over my financial situation. I told him I felt financially behind for someone my age and we devised a plan. I had saved enough money for a down payment on a small condo. With my permission, he took that money and leveraged it three times over. That is, he invested the money in stocks, used the stock as collateral, and borrowed again on sixty percent of the value to purchase more stocks. He did this twice over again and in effect the investment was doubled through leverage. His promise was that he was going to quadruple my money in a year. Of course I was very excited. I would have enough money for an excellent condo down payment, a new car and the beginning of a good retirement fund. How hungry I was for this kind of security.

Less than a year after the investment disaster struck! The stocks went from six dollars to a dollar and the bank "called in the margin." I lost all my stock, and was in debt to the tune of three times the amount that I had saved. **A feeling of devastation and shock riveted through my soul.** I still remember sitting there with the banker, in denial that they were going to take my stock. Everything was surreal in the office. I was there but I wasn't there. "Please don't sell my stock," I heard myself saying. They had to in order to pay a part of my debt. It was all very hard to accept. All that hard earned money was gone and now I would have to spend years paying off the debt. I went from being above ground to being in a deep hole. My broker friend was unprofessional and wrong to do what he did and I was wrong to trust him. I had made him my financial god. I had to learn yet another lesson in life. Instead of being patient and letting my money grow slowly, I was greedy and gambled. I had ignored the advice of a man who was a financial success, my Dad. Furthermore, after searching the Bible for wisdom on finances I found an abundance of practical advice.

Don't risk money that you cannot afford to lose.

By the 3rd printing of this book, I had finally paid back the money I owed. I had learned to change my lifestyle and to live modestly and frugally. I was grateful for having being given the opportunity to learn about the principles of money success.

It Takes 20 Years To Become an Overnight Success

When I first started doing motivational seminars, I would barely mention my failures. My introducer would say that I had two university degrees, had spoken all over the world, had lived at the North Pole, flown jets, played Junior hockey, taught tennis professionally, started various seminar programs, and taught in a private school. People would look at me and say, "Wow, I feel like I haven't started living yet compared to you." I was untouchable. This was a very safe place for me to be.

I could stand in front of an audience and no one could question my credibility because I was so "successful" as given by my list of accomplishments. Yet I had a host of failures under my belt. I have learned that what people really want and need is authenticity. Having associated with so many different types of people, I learned that millionaires have as many problems as the poor do. People who look good in public and have all the trappings of success may in fact have a good deal of misery in their lives. People who seem to have it all together, seldom do. I was just like the people in my audiences. They had successes and failures. I had successes and failures. We can't hide behind our failures and we can't gloat about our successes. Life is a process and each new day is an opportunity to begin anew and to make a contribution.

I am not one of those people you read about in the news who became an overnight success. As this book was being written I was still on a journey to succeed. There are very few "overnight successes." My mentor Zig Ziglar took twenty years to become a world famous speaker. Stephen Covey's book was a workbook that took years to develop into a world's best seller. It takes years to become the manager in your department, to learn a language, to be a better wife, husband or parent. Success is not what it appears to be. It is the ongoing development of one's character. It's not an end in itself but a process. As you read the ensuing chapters and apply the principles to your situation, you too will be on a journey. Discovering what success really is will be the next part of that journey. When you understand the nature of success, you'll realize that you have way more success in your life than you may understand. Read on!

Chapter 2 — Summary

Experience Pain - Gain Wisdom

- Sometimes you have to swallow your pride in order to succeed.
- You can seek after victories in one part of your life while you are getting over failures in other areas. Success is not an all or none deal.
- There is good and bad in all seminar programs, books and people. You must learn to discern and do what is right, not what is easiest or most joyful.
- Be careful not to rely heavily or idolise one person. You're asking for trouble.
- Never ever put all your financial eggs in one basket. Risk only what you can afford to lose.
- Life is a process and each new day is an opportunity to begin anew.
- It takes 20 years to become an overnight success.

Stay Fired Up!

3

GET THE RIGHT SUCCESS

My friend Jeff Gunther says, "nothing succeeds like a budgie without teeth." Wait for it. OK, I'll break it up for you. Succeeds can also be sounded out as, "sucks seeds." It's a corny joke that pokes fun at the old saying, "Nothing succeeds like success." But in essence, the saying *is* profound. It seems that people who create small successes over time turn them into bigger successes and their life takes on a momentum of success. My personal roller coaster of success and failure caused me to launch an investigation about what success *really* was. I wanted to find out if true happiness existed. Was success defined by the culture, the person, or by God? Was I seeking success in the wrong way, or was the failing aspect of my journey all a part of the equation? I wanted to know why some people were more successful than others. Why did they have more money, quality friends, better health, and nicer kids? Why are some people so darned happy all the time? Why are they excited about life?

Was it intelligence? No, I discovered many intelligent people who were depressed, poverty-stricken, or in jail. In fact, a high percentage of major criminals fall into the genius category. Was it luck or fate? No, I discovered that those people who were lucky had worked at getting lucky by having right principles, that is, right thinking, right speaking and right actions. I discovered that "lucky" people were the kind to turn the bad into good. They turned their disappointments into victories. Like the oyster, successful people turned irritations into pearls. Instead of getting ground down, they were getting polished up.

> *I'm a great believer in luck, and I find the harder I work, the more I have of it.*
>
> **THOMAS JEFFERSON (1743-1826)**
> **THIRD PRESIDENT OF THE U.S., PRINCIPAL**
> **AUTHOR OF THE DECLARATION OF INDEPENDENCE**

In their search for success, many people make the mistake of trying to be the best. This book might be misinterpreted as one that would incite you to outdo everyone else, to be better, higher, richer, or simply *the* best. Success is not about being *the* best; it is about being *your* best. You will never be *the* best because there will always be someone smarter, faster, better looking, funnier, stronger, or richer than you. Nevertheless, by following the same principles the best people do, you will grow to become the best person you can be. That is something to be happy and proud about. **When you are on the way to becoming your best, you can help others be their best.** Talk about a formula for successful living!

I like to organise my life by using something called "key areas." We will speak more about them in the goal-setting section, but for now I will use these key areas to expand the above question. What does it mean for you to be your best? Here are some suggestions. Take the time to think about each one and see if they apply to you. Envision yourself in each situation and "feel" it as if it has happened. Again, this is to excite your imagination. It is not an expectation but an ideal.

Spiritual

You wake up each morning excited about life. It is as if you were going on a vacation to Tahiti. You have unshakeable confidence in yourself. You have a strong and loving relationship with God. You love all of humanity, even your enemies. You harbour no resentment and forgive and forget easily. Going to bed is difficult because you are thrilled about life. You get over failures quickly and easily. You reflect, learn, and move on. You have a deep sense of inner peace.

Do these appear out of reach or too "pie in the sky?" Stay tuned!

Health

You have vibrant energy all day long. Your eyes shine and you radiate a positive energy everywhere around you. You are able to participate in any sport or adventure activity you wish. All the organs in your body are healthy and you have excellent eating habits. You are fit and toned.

Family: Parents

The relationship with your parents is one of absolute unconditional love; each time together is a joy and a blessing; you feel only unconditional love. They recognise and acknowledge in you all your positive qualities and trust that you are working on your negative ones. You honour your parents and are thankful for what they have done for you. You accept them for who they are.

Family: Immediate

You and your spouse are deeply and securely in love with each other. Your love is not based on filling a void in your life but on a free full self-expression. Your children are a joy even in the toughest of times. You go through traumas, but the undercurrent of your relationship is profound love.

Note: Take a minute to monitor your reactions to some of these ideals. If you are saying things like, "This is impossible," or "There's no way it could happen," then remember when you opened this book, you began a new journey; you are breaking out of the box. Start watching your reactions and get excited about these possibilities. Let's continue.

Wealth

You live in the beautiful home of your dreams. You can freely provide for your family without worrying about money. You are able to take nice vacations. You enjoy giving money and time to your favourite charitable organisations. You own a boat or a cabin on a lake. You are able to help your family and friends with financial problems. You can afford to give your children the best education. You are able to provide the best of medical care for you and your family members.

Career

You cannot wait to get to work each day. Your work activity excites you. Work is challenging and rewarding. You've become known for a very special contribution or expertise in your company or business.

Social

People love being with you. While you don't need the company of others, you thoroughly enjoy their friendship. You spend time with those who are honest, authentic, caring, fun loving, and adventurous about life.

The above words were designed to provoke or incite you to really take a look at your definition of success. Has your life been lulled into a comfortable dullness, or is each new day an exciting adventure? World-renowned speaker Brian Tracy certainly appears to be "successful." He went from being a dishwasher to a business consultant and accomplished speaker. He communicates in several languages, is in excellent physical condition, and has a very loving family. In his tape series, *The Psychology of Success*, he listed the criteria which psychologists use to define success. Those criteria are:

#1 Peace of mind, namely freedom from fear, anger, and guilt.

#2 Good health and high energy.

#3 Intimate relationships that are long-term, loving, and mature.

#4 Financial freedom.

#5 Commitment to worthy goals and ideals.

#6 The feeling of personal fulfilment or self-actualisation, that we are becoming everything we are capable of.

If you could go through the list and give a positive response to all of these, you may perhaps call yourself successful. Success can also be defined as, *"the progressive realisation of a person's worthwhile predetermined goals."* We seem to have a need to make a difference, to contribute, to be heard, and to achieve. Notice that success in these terms has no sense of permanence. That is, you cannot be successful once and for all. **Success is an ongoing process that will continue until the day you die.**

William Cooke, the author of *Success, Motivation and the Scriptures* stated that success involves: *Being able to accept yourself, knowing you are on the winning team, winning daily victories, getting along with others, achieving the maximum that can be achieved with what God has given you.*

I love the following quotes on success. Each time I read them, I feel renewed to go out and take action toward my goals, my dreams, and my passions. They come from people who have experienced a great deal of living.

> *Success is going from failure to failure without loss of enthusiasm.*
>
> **—WINSTON CHURCHILL**

> *You can have everything in life you want, if you will just help enough people get what they want.*
>
> **—ZIG ZIGLAR**

> *Success is much more than a matter of achieving the right things; it is also a matter of being the right person.*
>
> **—WILLIAM H. COOKE**

What is success in the world? I would say it consists of four simple things-to live a lot, to love a lot, to laugh a lot, and from it all, to learn a lot.

—**RICHARD J. NEEDHAM**

Success is failure with the dirt brushed off.

—**MAMIE MCCULLOUGH**

The price of success is hard work, dedication to the job at hand, and the determination that whether we win or lose, we have applied the best of ourselves to the task at hand.

—**VINCE LOMBARDI**

The person who succeeds is not the one who holds back, fearing failure, nor the one who never fails, but rather the one who moves on in spite of failure.

—**CHARLES SWINDOLL**

I attribute my success to this: I never gave or took an excuse.

—**FLORENCE NIGHTINGALE**

To be successful, you have to believe you can change the conditions in your life. You have to get out of the back seat of someone else's car and get behind your own steering wheel. You can't daydream your hopes into reality. You have to consider the options, reach decisions, take steps, and make moves. Make things happen.

—**BUCK ROGERS**

The measure of my success is my relationship with God as demonstrated by the visible fruits of the spirit, namely, love, joy, peace, patience, kindness, goodness, faithfulness, gentleness, and self-control.

—**DAVE PHILLIPS**

Success is not reserved for the talented. It is not for the high I.Q., in the gifted birth, not in the best equipment, not even in ability. Success is almost totally dependent upon drive, focus, and persistence.

—**DR. DENIS WAITLEY**

Sales trainer Tommy Hopkins talks about how one day he was going through a tollbooth. The attendant took the toll from the limousine driver and in a voice filled with sincere passion and enthusiasm said, "Have a beautiful day!" Then he stuck his head in, halfway toward the back of the limousine, and said with the same level of enthusiasm, "And you too, sir, you have a beautiful day." The limousine drove on and Mr. Hopkins exclaimed, "Something isn't right here! Pull over." He then walked back to the tollbooth attendant. Mr. Hopkins asked the man why he was so enthusiastic. With the same exuberance, the man explained that he was healthy, had a beautiful wife and children, his house was almost paid off, he was nearing his goal for retirement, and all day long he had the privilege of taking people's money.

Most people would look at a job as menial as a tollbooth attendant and conclude that it was a dead end. But when you look at the definition of success, the man met the criteria. He had a worthwhile goal, excellent health, wonderful relationships, financial security, and peace of mind. Some of you are thinking that you could never be happy with such small goals. That's fine, but one must remember that to this man, those goals and that lifestyle may have represented ultimate prosperity and success. We get into so much trouble when we try to compare ourselves with others.

Studies have shown that people who suddenly inherit or win large sums of money quit their jobs and spend the whole lot of it within a year or two. They are no happier than they were before, and in fact, they may even slide into depression. The famous television show, "*Who Wants to be a Millionaire.*" epitomizes our culture. People always talk about how happy they would be if they could just win a million dollars. I have a friend of a friend who was in that position. Oh, what a glorious day it was when that money came into his family. He was relieved of many headaches, able to pay for his house, and take better care of their friends and family. But money could not take care of his health challenges or relationship struggles. Money could not bring him the happiness he so desperately yearned for.

I know what you are thinking; you honestly believe in your heart that money would really take care of all your problems. Consider another point of view. Would you be happier winning a million dollars or earning a million dollars? Your instinctive answer might be that winning it would make you happier. Suppose your wish has been granted to you. At last you could do all those things that you dreamed about.

Question: Who would you have become in the winning of the million? Answer: the same person you were before.

People who *earn* money also value it more and become proud of themselves in the process. It is whom we have *become* that counts the most, and becoming takes time.

Be a 747

Human beings are like a 747 aircraft. The designers of this magnificent piece of technology tell us that the aircraft wears out faster by sitting on the ground than when it is flying in the heavens. Isn't that ironic? One would think it would last longer if there was less stress on the airframe and parts. But engineers built the 747 to fly. It was built to perform. It was built to serve. The wings of the aircraft are less stressed when they're performing lift. The ball bearings in the turbine engines are lubricated when they're turning. The wonderful news is that this principle is true for human beings. You will last longer and enjoy life more if you learn to fly in your own way.

People who have succeeded financially over time have developed their character along the way. They suffered hardships. They outlived rejection. They learned how to develop faith in the face of evidence that would have them quit. They developed their character, which became a foundation for their success. Have you ever noticed that when a house or a high-rise is being built, it seems to take forever to build the foundation? When I worked in construction many years ago, I started as a labourer two stories below the ground level. It seemed like I was down in those water-filled ditches forever, carrying lumber up and down and laying concrete. Huge I-beams were pounded deep into the earth to solidify the foundation; everything else evolved around those beams. Once we finished the basement parking lot, life was much easier. There was no more mucking around. We had earned our way out of the pit. Building character is like that. You learn lesson after lesson, and sometimes it feels like you are "in the muck." The pain of learning can really hurt, but you must learn. And when you have learned, like the I-beams, your character will be deeply rooted with integrity and wisdom. As a result, when it comes to money, you will have learned how to make it and keep it. With your relationships, you will be able to endure the hard times and come back with forgiveness, love, and compassion.

Examine your level of excitement for living. Do you awaken scared, resigned, and cynical or do you wake up and say, "All right! It's another beautiful day! I get to really go for it today! I can't wait to get out there and make a difference with everyone I meet!" Humans have a need to achieve, to grow, to improve, and to make a difference. By looking in the right places, you too will find success based on rock solid values.

Yesterday is history and tomorrow a mystery.

UNKNOWN

Today is God's gift, that's why it's called the PRESENT!

UNKNOWN

Carpe Diem (Latin for seize the day!)

Today is the first day of the rest of your life.

UNKNOWN

This is the day the Lord has made! Let us rejoice and be glad in it!

THE BIBLE-PSALM 118:24

Chapter 3 — Summary

Get the Right Success

- Success is being your best, not the best.
- Success involves many different areas of your life including spiritual, health, family, wealth, career and social.
- Success is the progressive realisation of a worthwhile goal.
- Success is accepting yourself.
- Success involves achieving the best you can with what God has given you.
- Success involves hard work and determination.
- Success involves persistence.
- Success is not your status.
- Success is the development of your character.
- Success involves seeking wisdom first.
- Success takes time and patience.

Stay Fired Up!

4

FIND WISDOM AT ALL COSTS

Over the years, I have experienced many people who often appeared to have the trappings of success—a nice home, a car, a spouse, 2.3 kids, but when I looked at a deeper level, they were living lives of quiet desperation. Their marital relationship was mere co-habitation, they barely saw their kids, they did their job more out of duty than passion, their health was failing, and so on. That's when I started wondering about the "secrets" of success. I use the word secrets because if they were not, wouldn't everyone be following them?

You have an advantage over 90 percent of the population. Your advantage is that most people have chosen to close their minds off to these secrets but you have chosen to read a book like this to access some of them. The secrets I'm about to share with you have been passed on down through the ages, since the beginning of time and used by many successful men and women. All that you need to uncover these secrets are eyes to see , ears to hear, and an open mind. There is a famous story in the world's best selling book about King Solomon that illustrates the significance of this chapter. God held him in high regard and told him that he could have anything he wanted. This was a fantastic opportunity for Solomon. This day and age, many people would be inclined to say, "Well Lord, can we start with a fine new home, and the new Lexus is looking pretty good, and could you fix my spouse please, and I'd love a promotion and a new boss at work. In fact, how about handing me over the company so it can be run the right way? I would also like a condo down south, a ski chalet, and a private aircraft. Oh and would you please fix my teenage son. I think that's about it. Thank you very much, Lord."

Solomon, however, did not make that kind of request. Speaking to the Lord, he asked, "Give your servant a discerning heart to govern your people and to distinguish between right and wrong." He asked only for wisdom to serve the people as King. In the ensuing years Solomon was to be considered the wisest man in the world. He was respected for his ability to rule and to make good decisions. He learned the secrets of success. He was hungry for wisdom. Oh, and by the way, he also ended up being the richest person to have ever lived. The words "wisdom and wealth" became associated with the name of King Solomon.

Long before I started this book, I developed an insatiable desire for wisdom. I had already discovered some secrets to happiness and success in the areas of health, wealth, and relationships that had made a profound difference in my life. I was happier and more comfortable in my shoes. I was more at peace and more confident in myself and in the future. I learned these secrets from a variety of sources such as my parents, books, audiocassette tapes, teachers, mentors, television, movies, friends and the Bible. I sought wisdom everywhere I could. I had become a sponge for knowledge, soaking it up at every available opportunity, and because I was open to change and honest about myself, I did receive important lessons on wisdom.

I wasn't always open to wisdom however. I was a typical teenager who really couldn't understand how my parents had become so successful when they didn't seem to know much about life. I spent a great deal of time trying to "enlighten" them as to what life was *really* about. After all, they were raised in the "olden days." As I grew older, I was amazed to discover how wise my parents had become in such a short amount of time! (That's humour if you missed it.)

Many people are busy protecting their lives from outside influences, especially in the realm of personal growth. They are more committed to *being right* about themselves and their views than they are about accepting something that will make a positive difference for them. On one hand, this attitude makes sense. If someone tells you that you have been wrong, possibly all your life, it invalidates that part of your life. It says you were wrong and you've been wrong for a long time. It's an affront to a person's character. People have a very powerful subconscious desire not to be wrong. Being *right* validates who they are. People like this stagnate as life passes them by. Assess yourself and ask the question, **"Is being right more important than being my best?"**

If you've ever seen the movie *Top Gun,* Maverick (Tom Cruise) had to eject after going into a flat spin while flying in a mock aerial dogfight. Tragically, he lost his navigator in the ejection. Later he was assigned to fight in another real dogfight, but when he reached the site he could not "engage." The thoughts of fear were overriding the thought of victory. The knowledge and skills were there, but the wisdom was still to be learned. In this case, the wisdom was that in aerial dog fighting people die. But fighter pilots have a duty. Life goes on. You can run away from your experiences or you can learn from them. Where lessons are concerned there are occasions where *you* don't want to "engage" because you know there may be impending pain or risk of failure. Human beings do more to avoid pain than to gain pleasure. Pleasure is blissful, whereas pain is awful. But if you are waiting around and avoiding life because you are afraid of pain, you will certainly miss out on life's most important lessons...and excitement!

> *The trouble with advice is that you can't tell if it's good or bad until you've taken it.*
>
> **—FRANK TYGER**

Most of us have empathy for this quote full of irony. We have accepted advice which we thought was wise and then later discovered that it really wasn't wise at all, or the advice wrong. As you read in chapters one and two, I learned some very big lessons because I put my faith in the wrong people. One of the interesting characteristics of advice seeking is that we sometimes go after it hoping to get a confirmation of our own already formed opinions or desires. When someone has expressed an idea different to our own, we thank him or her politely and go elsewhere looking for agreement. Finally, we find the advice that agrees with our view or idea and become so excited about it that we forget to look where the advice came from. It may be that the person who dispensed the advice is not an authority in the matter but our opinion of them overrides our established values and principles. Follow seemingly good advice from the wrong person and you have a recipe for disaster.

> *Most of us ask for advice when we know the answer but want a different one.*
>
> **—IVERN BELL**

We live in the information age. Many people today are seeking knowledge but not wisdom. What good is information if you don't have the discipline and wisdom to use it? For example, if you learn all about investing prudently but have foolish spending habits then what good is the information? If you do a course on how to run a successful business, but you sleep in until ten in the morning and procrastinate, what's the use? If you read the six keys to successful relationships but are unwilling to apologise to your spouse, how will you grow? Never before have we lived in such a society where personal growth and development information is so readily available and yet the moral and ethical fabric of society is eroding. The Internet is a cornucopia of information. People are buying computers in record numbers. They are depriving themselves of sleep and using up valuable work time in order to get the next tantalising piece of information. Gathering information over the Internet is similar to watching television. After a while, you just get "zoned out." Nothing has changed in your life except that you have more information. Many identify their worth with how much information they can expound. People are so proud to be able to tell you the statistics of a baseball player or how the stock market is doing, but ignore the important aspects of life. Seek wisdom before you seek knowledge. Clearly understand why you are seeking that knowledge. Have a vision and a goal plan. Then you can find the knowledge to support your plan.

It seems that the older we get the less we want to learn or the less open we are to learning. Many of us stopped learning when we graduated from school. We are forced to learn new technologies and skills for our jobs, but how much time are we devoting to being a better human being, a more successful person, a better parent, a more considerate friend, colleague, or leader? As part of my own learning process, I make it a point to speak to the elderly at my church. They have so much wisdom to impart. I see it as stopping at a gold mine of wisdom and having someone fill up my bucket. One day I had a delightful experience. On a previous Sunday, I had told one of the ladies how beautiful she looked. This woman, about 80 years young, was reticent to accept my compliment. I thought nothing more of the communication and went on to speak with others. On the following Sunday, she came up to me with deep concern in her eyes and apologised for her behaviour the Sunday before. I didn't understand why she had to apologise. She explained that it was very ungracious of her not to accept my compliment, and that it must be an issue of hers that she should work on. I was impressed because here was a respected elder of the church, full of grace and wisdom, and yet was still willing to improve herself. That made me appreciate Grace McPhee even more and it made me realize that the search for wisdom is never ending.

I also have two other good friends Stan and Ruth Cummings who are 83 and 79 respectively at the time of this book. Each day they are engulfed in reading the Bible, several publications, and they have numerous books on the go. They attend lectures of various kinds, are on committees for church and state and at the same time are open to personal improvement suggestions from anyone. I've often heard them say, "thank you for correcting me."

If your neighbour had a beautiful garden, and *you* wanted a beautiful garden, would you not go over and ask, "Hey, good neighbour, how do you create such a beautiful garden?" But many do not ask, and for a variety of reasons. They are too shy, too embarrassed about their own garden, they think they already know how, or are simply too proud to ask. This is unfortunate. People want their life to be a beautiful garden and yet they are unwilling to seek the knowledge and wisdom. Rest assured that there are gardens *you* are trying to cultivate and make beautiful, but you lack sufficient knowledge or wisdom, or worse, you aren't aware that the knowledge or wisdom exists. But here you are reading this book. By doing this, you have made a commitment to change your life, to improve it, to overcome an adversity, to become more, to serve others better and to grow. Congratulations! May your garden flourish in beauty and usefulness.

Chapter 4 — Summary

Find Wisdom At All Costs

- Change from being right to being your best.
- Gaining wisdom can be painful but avoiding it can be more painful.
- Be careful about following advice that merely aligns with your desires but not your values.
- Find the right sources to acquire wisdom.
- Seek wisdom until your last breath.

Stay Fired Up!

5

GET THE EQUATION RIGHT HOPE + FAITH + ACTION = SUCCESS

I loved hearing my Mom's stories from her childhood. Although we had heard them over and over, every time a story was told, we were able to touch a piece of her life and grow in intimacy with her. My mother grew up in a very poor family in Winnipeg, Manitoba, Canada. Her father left the family when she was very young and my grandmother had to raise five daughters on her own through very tough times. How tough was it? Tragically, my grandmother couldn't afford to feed them and the daughters were sent to foster homes at various times. However, for the majority of the time, in order to keep custody of those daughters, my grandmother worked at the telephone company by day and as a waitress at the racetrack by night. She did this day after day, week in and week out.

It was such a contrast to my middle class upbringing in a military family. Moving every three or four years certainly had its drawbacks, but one of the perquisites of it was free air travel on some really cool aircraft. How excited I used to get, as we would board the C130 Hercules aircraft in Trenton, Ontario or Sherwater, Nova Scotia, to fly to Winnipeg where Granny lived. As a young boy, I was innocent about the strength of Granny's character. All I saw was a fun-loving grandmother who loved me and who took me to the Pancake House where I could have strawberry pancakes for breakfast, and then strawberry shortcake for dessert right after. I use to believe that's where heaven was.

In my late teens, as I became more understanding and appreciative of people, I saw something interesting about my grandmother. She was stubborn and she was a dreamer! For a number of years, she had been travelling to Kona, Hawaii for vacation. Besides her day job, she would also earn extra money babysitting and knitting blankets. She loved Hawaii, and her dream was to one day live in island paradise. Most people thought this was a rather bold idea. How could she afford it? She was nearing retirement and worked at the telephone company, which wasn't exactly the best paying position. As well, the equity in her house in Winnipeg did not bode well for house values in Hawaii. There were some very logical reasons why this was an impossible dream, but Granny thought otherwise!

On December 25, 1979, I got off an aircraft in Kona, Hawaii with my sister. There at the airport to greet us was my Grandmother and many other family members. It was a gorgeous sunny day and the journey along the coastline was stunning as the palm trees swayed in the warm winds. The ocean was glorious as the white capped waves provided contrast to the richness of the blues and greens. You can guess where we drove? My grandmother's condo was only a hundred feet from the ocean, where the powerful waves crashed against black lava rocks. There was a modern swimming pool in the courtyard surrounded by stately palm trees and it was all simply brilliant!

She had done it. Against great odds, she had done it. With stubborn determination, with unrelenting hope and faith, she had fulfilled her dream. It was a wonderful paradise and a dream come true! What a joy it was to be with her in Hawaii, and how delighted she was to show off her grandchildren to the many friends she had acquired.

Granny's dream, like all things, would have its ending. In 1985, I visited my Grandmother back in Winnipeg. As a Canadian living in USA, she was unable to afford the medical bills for the care required for her illness. The cancer in her back and neck was terminal, and she was in great pain. What a contrast it was between then and my previous visit. I was unable to attend Granny's funeral but I did have the honour of writing her eulogy. In it, I remembered my Grandmother as a tremendous role model and a great player in the game of life. She was a visionary, and she knew about hope. She was a living example of hope in action.

Hope Is the Source of Joy

One of the most critical aspects of successful living is the ability to have hope. It is amazing how just a little bit of hope can sustain a human being. But how does one find hope? When you lose it, where and how can you get it back? Why are some so filled with hope and enthusiasm for living, while others are repressed and depressed?

Perhaps it can be said that our inability to experience hope is a result of how deeply we have let negativity etch a groove into our mind. We sure didn't start out feeling hopeless. If we have let negative events, bad experiences, and the opinions of others form and shape our view of the world, it becomes a battle to enjoy life and to overcome misery. There are many people who have suffered horrific experiences in their past, yet they have flourished while others have not. Why is this so? The dictionary defines hope as, *1. A feeling that what is wanted will happen. 2. Desire accompanied by anticipation or expectation.* (Webster's New World Dictionary) Victor Frankl, who was tortured and witnessed the horrors of the Nazi brutality talked of how man can take everything away from you except your ability to decide to interpret the situation and circumstance in a way that leads toward life or death. He said that the one thing that kept him alive was having the vision that he would some day be alive and in front of audiences to tell his story. He knew about hope.

> *Everything can be taken from a man but one thing: the last of his freedoms—to choose one's attitude in any given set of circumstances, to choose one's way.*
>
> **—VICTOR FRANKL,** *MAN'S SEARCH FOR MEANING*

What about you and hope? Is your relationship in ruins, your heart broken, never to love again? Are you financially destitute, whereby you've lost it all or you feel way behind in your net worth as I once was. Is your body not functioning properly. Have you lost a good friend, either through conflict, or even death. Do you have a boss whom you despise and who treats you like you're in third grade. Does your life seem monotonous and dull. Do you feel you have achieved all your dreams and are wondering what's next. Is it possible you don't like yourself very much and have even thought of ending it all at times. You, by all appearances, are successful with a fine job, executive position, and wonderful spouse and children, but feel empty inside. If you are looking at your own situation thinking it's hopeless, do not lose heart. Whatever your case, remember there is always someone else worse off than you but they still keep going. History is full of remarkable examples of how people were able to overcome adversity and triumph over it. So will you!

I have read many books that have made a significant impact on my life. Why were they so effective? Each time I read a quality book on understanding life, I had a sense of renewal. I shed whatever went against hope in my life and filled up with inspiration. I recharged and reprogrammed my inner computer. You too can do this with books, tapes, videos, seminar programs, music, and mentors. I believe that one of the most important aspects of hope is setting things into motion. Hope becomes alive when you propel yourself into action. What good is hope if it's nothing but an inert feeling within your blissful but idle existence? Perhaps this is where faith comes in. Hope is tied in with faith. Faith is what helps you "believe" that the hope can be fulfilled.

Rachel Keung, a wise friend of mine, says that faith is intangible, but you believe in it so much that you trust in it and when you trust in it you stand behind it and live it. "It's hopeless without faith," says Rachel. This rings loud and significant in my mind. When you look up the he word "faith" in the world's best selling book it says:

Faith is being sure of what we hope for and certain of what we do not see.

– HEBREWS 11:1 -THE BIBLE

The dictionary defines faith as follows, "Unquestionable belief; complete trust, confidence, or reliance." (Webster's New World Dictionary.) That confidence and reliance will move you forward in your life. Faith will be the foundation of your drive and your power source.

It is often difficult to have faith, however, because you can't see it. You cannot physically view the realisation of your goals, your ideal wife, your wonderful home, a happy heart, and a successful business. You can't see it literally, but you can see it in your mind's eye. This is where the power of visualisation comes in. When you develop a powerful vision and an exciting set of goals, you will see in your mind's eye what you want to do. When you believe it at a deep level, your hope will be strengthened. You will be inspired, and that inspiration will cause you to take action and to accomplish. How do you find the faith to strengthen your hope? The good news is that you can find it by listening to a good speaker, talking to a friend, reading a good book, experiencing a life changing event, thinking about some of your past successes or by praying. Also, you must think about your failures and recognise that you did live through them and you did learn from them. By hearing, seeing, and reading about the successes of others who have overcome adversity, you will be uplifted and moved into action. Know that you will have few successes and many failures, and this will build your character. The more your character is built, the more hope you will develop. By suffering, you will persevere and by persevering you will build character. By building character, you will inspire more hope. Examine these statements and see if you agree:

1. **Hope plus faith lead to action.**
2. **Action leads to failure or success.**
3. **Failure leads to knowledge and the building of character strength.**
4. **Success also leads to building character.**
5. **Character strength and knowledge lead to success.**
6. **Success leads to confidence.**
7. **Confidence leads to more action.**

The key to success is having faith and taking action. Faith in action will make your life rich. My main objective with this entire book is that by the time you finish it, you will have an unquestionable belief and confidence in your ability to succeed in every area of your life. No matter where you are right now, no matter how bad things seem, no matter how far away your goals may appear, and no matter how impossible something is, you can succeed and you will succeed.

What do you think is the main reason why people won't take action? Take a minute to think about that and write some of your thoughts down.

____

____

____

____

The main reason why people won't take action is because they are hope-less and faith-less. They don't believe that by taking action the desired result will occur. They won't exercise because they don't really believe they'll lose weight, or they don't have the confidence that they have the strength to carry on. They don't express love because they don't believe it will pay off, or they think the risk of rejection is too high. They won't work harder at their job because they don't believe it will bring returns. And the biggest danger of all is that after many months, years, and even decades, they become absolutely "right" about that hope. They are blinded to their own magnificence because for years they have proven that life offers only so much. They have lost hope.

Are *you* living that kind of life, a life of quiet desperation? Don't be too quick to answer. Your instant reaction to the question may be your ego covering up your fears. Parts of your life may be working well, while you have buried the desperation in other areas. Think about those mornings when you did not want to get out of bed. I have had mornings like this. In arising without hope, you have to start the mundane cycle of living all over again. To live for eight to nine hours in psychological pain awaiting the end of the day is tormenting. And, if you think it doesn't affect your family, you are misled. On the other hand, some of us can't wait to get to work in order to avoid the pain of being at home and that too is distressing.

When I was in my early twenties, I courted a nurse named Christina. She was overflowing with life and I was in love with her exuberance and her warmth. One night while having a quiet evening together, I asked her why she was this way. She said that by working as a nurse in intensive care she saw first hand the many people who had worked their fingers to the bone, retired at age 65, got sick and died without really enjoying the fruits of their labours. This explained her philosophy of living each day to the fullest. Yes we must work hard and this is good for us. But at the same time, it is important to strive toward what we love. When we find what we love, we make a greater contribution to the world because we are operating in our gifting area. While you're exploring to find what you love, try to enjoy as much as possible what you are currently doing. When you can have a "service to others" mindset, time will pass and you'll smile more.

Keep a President's Attitude

What if you knew that you were going to become the president of the company you worked at? It doesn't matter if you are delivering the office mail in your company's high-rise. If you *knew*, and you knew that you knew you were to become president, do you think you would do things differently? I'll bet you would be more consistent in your deliveries to ensure perfection. I'll bet you would develop a system that would guarantee timeliness. I'll bet you would find ways to cut costs and increase efficiency. With the extra time you had, you would probably help someone else in their work. Maybe you would improve the appearance of your area or invent more time saving measures. Maybe you would send some cards of encouragement to those in the company that you experienced as in need of a boost.

Some might emphatically say, "I don't think so." You're thinking you would take a nap with your extra time and maybe request a salary raise to make up for what you did for the company. You have invested extra time and effort so you should be rewarded. Well, you are probably right. You should be rewarded and recognised. But do you think that if you continued with this kind of zeal and behaviour, someone would notice? I can hear some of you thinking again, "I do all that, and I still don't get noticed." To this I say, "Keep going with your president's attitude." You must think that it's your company, and you're just going to do what it takes to make it great. Can you see and feel the difference? If you have the right heart and the right attitude, you *will* make your way to the top. You cannot help it. It is the law of life. And if the system you're in will not recognize you, then find a place that will, but don't' complain about where you're at.

> *Give me a stock clerk who wants to work, and I'll give you a person who'll make history. Give me a person who doesn't want to work, and I'll give you a stock clerk.*
>
> **—J.C. PENNY**

What about your health? What if you knew that you were going to live until you were a hundred and that your years would all be fruitful? What if you knew you were going to be needed to run the company or the Grandparents Volunteer Society in your town? What if at the age of 88, a company wanted you to sit on their board of directors, and you had six grandchildren who really loved and needed you? Do you think you would take care of yourself differently? Would you stop smoking and maybe drink less coffee? Would you exercise a little more? Would you lose the weight?

Would you stop fretting? Would you live life with more integrity? Of course you would because you would be filled with hope and vision.

What if you *knew* you were going to have a wonderful marriage, that your love would deepen each day, month, and year, that you would experience the kind of joy you only read about? Would you be different in your relationship? Would you speak to your spouse more lovingly? Would you say goodbye differently? Would you forgive faster? Would you be more considerate? Would you honour your spouse more? Of course you would. Some couples run into the chicken and egg syndrome thinking, "I would be nicer to my spouse if she or he would only be nicer to me." This pattern of thinking will only contribute to a vicious cycle. Only your hope, your vision and faith will enable you to act positively despite the negative circumstances.

You may have heard the saying "fake it 'til you make it." If it is difficult for you to create a positive vision for your life, maybe fake it for a week, or a year, or even five years. Imagine that you have already achieved what you wanted, that you are already the kind of person who has found that success. You will be amazed at the results. Note that you must commit to a time period. Why not start off with a week? Create a wonderful vision for a relationship, your health, wealth or career, and act in accordance with your vision. Just choose one area. Keep a journal and watch what happens. You may find that you are doing way more than you think to exacerbate your problems by living out a negative vision. Living with hope and faith will also help you to live in the "now." The reason is that when you have faith in your future, you need not be concerned about it. All you need to do is make your plan every day and go, go, go.

Appreciate What You Do Have

Developing the ability to appreciate what you *do* have, while remaining hopeful of better things, is critically important. You have had mornings when you couldn't wait to begin your day. Maybe you were going on vacation, you had a date, or you had an important business presentation. You had great hope for the day. The key to a peaceful mind is striking a balance with hope for the future on one side, and enjoying and appreciating the present on the other. My older sister Gale continues to remind me, "Take it one day at a time."

Some people give those who have succeeded less credit by saying: They must have had inner strength, they must have been more disciplined, or they must have been born with the ability to overcome adversity. These statements are untrue. Perhaps they may have had the benefit of an excellent upbringing but many people who have gone through tough times had to get tough. In ninety-nine percent of cases involving crises or failure turned to success, individuals learned to persevere through faith. They developed character strength and hope for the future.

Did you know that 52% of CEOs of Fortune 500 companies are from lower-middleclass or poor families, and 80% of the millionaires in America are first generation millionaires? Did you know that 75% of the three hundred world class leaders in a recent study were raised in poverty, had been abused as children or had a serious physical disability. [Zig Ziglar-Over the Top-1997 P2]

It does not matter where you're at right now. I don't care if you're broke, battle fatigued, disabled, disgruntled, unmotivated, unmarried, overweight, overtaxed, alone, alarmed, unloved or undone, you can succeed, you will succeed and you must succeed! Keep the cycle of hope, faith and action going and it will happen for you. Yes, you are going to be a story that people will want to write about.

Chapter 5 — Summary

Get the Equation Right
Hope + Faith + Action= Success

- Hope plus faith leads to action.
- Action leads to failure and success.
- Failure leads to knowledge and the building of character strength.
- Character strength and knowledge lead to success.
- Success leads to confidence.
- Be a stubborn dreamer.
- We lose hope when we let negativity etch a groove in our mind.
- Take on a President's attitude.
- Keep a positive vision in your mind's eye.
- Appreciate today while you're working on tomorrow.

Stay Fired Up!

PART II

The Power of Your Mind

6

BELIEVE IN MOTIVATION

Zig Ziglar invited Dr. Forest Tennant, the number-one drug authority in America, to attend one of his four-hour seminars to determine the impact of hearing motivational words and ideas. Dr. Tennant ran blood tests on volunteers before and after the seminar. He discovered that endorphin and cortisol levels went up as much as 300 percent after a message of hope! (May 1997 Meetings and Conventions Magazine.) The effects lasted only a few hours, but the results were amazing. Dr. Tennant went on to say that a message of hope and success enthusiastically delivered creates excitement which floods the brain with endorphins, dopamine, serotonin (the self-esteem enhancer), norephinephrine, and other neurotransmitters. This proves that physiological change occurs when we are exposed to motivation. When we create or experience an empowering vision or hear motivating words, our brain responds to it. The brain is wired for encouragement and motivation. A message of hope and success creates excitement that makes us want to succeed.

How motivated are *you*? Have you ever been depressed? Have you ever been broke? Have you ever had your heart broken? Have you ever had too much month left at the end of the money? Have you ever been so anxious and strung out that you felt you could literally snap? Have you ever thought about ending it all? Have you ever been frustrated? Have you ever suffered guilt because you didn't do what you should have done, yet couldn't motivate yourself to do it? Most of us will have answered affirmatively to at least one of these questions. After all, we are human. The good news is that there *are* secrets to surviving these challenges and to living a life of success. You really can live a life of love, joy, patience, kindness, goodness, success, and even everlasting peace. But how do we find the motivation to find access all this?

One morning I woke up feeling depressed. I was falling short of reaching my goals and was in poor shape financially. I also badly wanted a family and children. Nearly all my friends were married and had children. It felt like they were getting on with their lives while I had a life of unfulfilled dreams.

And yet I felt ashamed about this attitude because I had so much going for me. I was perfectly healthy, lived in a beautiful home, had a great job, had a nice circle of friends, and was living in the paradise city of Vancouver, Canada. I was an excellent tennis player, golfer, skier, and belonged to a wonderful church. Still, I felt unfulfilled. I was looking at my life as a series of failures and lost opportunities. Most would have viewed my life as beautiful. Why would I be depressed?

On that morning I knew I had to get out of the house. I went over to a local coffee shop and bought a cup of java. There on top of the shelf with all the other merchandised products was a book written by the CEO of Starbucks, Howard Schultz. I picked it up, started reading and was unable to put the book down. One hour and four chapters later, I was totally inspired. I couldn't wait to get back to work. Something occurred to me that was far more important than the actual message communicated in the book. The most important realisation was that in the span of an hour, my brain wave patterns were transformed from depression to exhilaration. Black ink typed onto a piece of paper inspired me? Nothing had actually changed in my life except my thoughts. By allowing the writing inside a book to form a picture inside my head I changed the very direction of my thinking and therefore my actions for that day.

What if I had not read the book? I might have had a good day, but given the state of my mind at the time, it was unlikely. The book caused me to rush back and enthusiastically make numerous phone calls, write an article, create my first motivational T-shirt, work on a proposal, and ask a woman out for a date. In addition, I met six different people for business and social reasons and because of my inspired state, I helped *them* have a better day. The dull rainy day seemed much brighter. I was seeing the world through rose-coloured glasses, but they weren't glasses, they were my own eyes and thoughts. Everything was different that day because of my newly acquired attitude. *The* world was the same, but *my* world was different.

> *If you say you never had a chance, perhaps you never took a chance.*
>
> **—HOWARD SCHULTZ**

Positive changes brought about by external circumstances are exciting but short-lived. If someone on the street gives you a hundred-dollar bill or if you win the hockey pool, that's great. If someone smiles and wishes you a nice day, that's terrific. If you get a sales lead from a total stranger, praise the Lord. These changes in circumstances all evoke positive emotions that last anywhere from five minutes to a couple of days. As nice as they are, they are bonuses.

What about circumstances that can change your emotions in a *negative* way? A car may hit you on the way to work. Someone may be inconsiderate to you. Your proposal may be turned down. You may lose the sale even though the client verbally agreed the day before. How will you deal with that negativity? The key is to vow to address the negative circumstances with a positive mental attitude. Taking this approach to living is crucial because it gives you far more control. On the day I read Mr. Schultz's book, it was personal initiative that incited the actions. The woman didn't call me nor did anyone write that proposal. Personal initiative had an end result that made me feel good about my character. The most relevant lesson for me was that my life could be altered via a simple communication.

In my case, the author's message caused me to re-discover my aim in life. My purpose was and still is to inspire others, bring out the best in people, help people discover their passion and develop a vision, provide people with tools to succeed, help people live well and "finish well." It was good to be reminded of that. You too are receiving reminders from this book of your own magnificence and purpose.

> *Some men see things as they are and say 'why?' I dream of things that never were and say 'why not?'*
>
> —GEORGE BERNARD SHAW

In daily life, you can get enormous pressure from friends, family, and colleagues urging you to take the easy way and thus accept mediocrity. But when you really believe in yourself and in your dreams, you just have to do everything you possibly can to take control and make your vision a reality. No great achievement happens by luck. Getting back to my initial point, it was not the print that motivated me, but the fact that I was fortunate enough to read it, believe it, and take action. I was open enough to change my attitude that day, and consequently my life was changed forever. When you take any action it changes your life; the key is to keep taking the best actions and to learn from the wrong ones.

Watch Out For Analysis Paralysis

It is important to note that taking no action is in itself an action. Often it is the fear of the unknown followed by mental paralysis that prevents us from being proactive. Although you'll be inspired by the contents of this book, you'll also have to put in some work to fulfil its promises. As I mentioned at the beginning of the book, my first major communication program had a dramatic influence on me. It gave me new tools, new hope, and a new vision. I was so inspired by the first seminar, that I took another one right after that. I took a few more "actions" to change my life, but what I really wanted was some more of that "inspiration." So I did another seminar, and another, and then another. At the end of each seminar, I thought, "Okay, after this seminar, my life will be totally fixed. It will be perfect." I initially thought that being enlightened and inspired would take care of all the problems in my life and my success would just happen. Big Caution: It doesn't work that way! Life is a process. Success takes time, patience, and work – *your* time, *your* patience, and *your* work.

> *You can accomplish anything you wish that is not contradictory to the laws of God and man, provided you are willing to pay a price!*
>
> **—W. CLEMENT STONE**

No doubt this quote is inspiring. While reading this book there will be times when you will be inspired. You will feel nice inside. You will love yourself and everyone else more. I have experienced this kind of joy many times after listening to motivational tapes, watching movies, reading books, and praying. When you have elevated yourself sufficiently, you will be able to put yourself in this state often. However, what will give you the greatest benefit is taking action immediately. When you feel inspired, put the book down and do something constructive. Apologise to that guy you had a fight with three years ago. Call your mother and tell her how much you love her. Tell your spouse what a great lover he or she is. Apologise to your children for misjudging them. Plan an evening to create the new family rules. Thank your boss for challenging you. Plan your next family vacation. Clean out your closet. Take action now. Don't wait. Reading this book is futile if it doesn't get you into action. Begin changing your life today!

> *Our worth is determined by our deeds not by our good intentions.*
>
> **—OG MANDINO**

Does motivation work? Absolutely! Your brain and body are wired for it. Will you be highly motivated at all times? Of course not! When you are inspired about your dreams and goals, write them down. Later on I will show you how to design a plan and succeed with it based on your commitment. **Inspiration is short term. Commitment is long term.** The purpose of this book is to help you bring out the best in you, your children, your company, and anyone you associate with. To take the right action you must have goals. To have goals you must understand what success is to you. You must recognise what your beliefs are and that if your beliefs are misguided or unclear you will find life very difficult to live. You will grab on to those beliefs that are passed on to you by your environment or circumstance. Invariably, this will get you into trouble. Ask yourself this: Is society succeeding? Are we progressing? Beliefs must come from an active choosing of what you know deep in your heart and soul to be true.

Chapter 6 — Summary

Believe in Motivation

- Your body and mind are wired for motivation.
- You can deal with any negative circumstance with a positive mental attitude.
- Learn from wrong actions and keep trying to take best actions.
- Inspiration is short term but commitment is long term.
- Commit to what you know is good and right...and do it now!

Stay Fired Up!

7

DON'T BELIEVE YOUR BELIEFS

Some time ago, I was promoting my training programs to Canadian Airlines. I had an appointment with the director of training and while waiting I met his assistant Sonia Halbert. In speaking with her I discovered that she was "the one." Let me explain. In July 1992, Canadian Airlines was about to be taken over by its competitor, Air Canada. Sonia refused to believe that her company, a company that prided itself on its service, would be dissolved forever. She knew that many would lose their jobs and that airline prices would climb as a result of the monopoly that would be created with only one major airline carrier in Canada. Sonia made numerous inquiries about how to prevent this catastrophe, but the responses were consistently the same. "There's nothing we can do." and "It's too late to do anything." Others in the company were too busy or too complacent to do anything. They knew they didn't have the power to do anything about the situation or they were afraid to ruffle feathers in their department. Sonia persisted and asked one of the service quality managers if she could have permission to start an employee initiative to save the company. Can you imagine this? What nerve, what gall, what courage! After some insistence, the manager relented by saying, "I don't know how you're going to do this, but go ahead." Sonia sent her message to employees across the nation urging them to save the company. In short order they were sending cheques as their pledge to save the airline. Sonia then met with a small group of volunteers in Toronto and arranged rallies of Canadian Airlines employees across Canada in August 1992. At the rallies, postcards were handed out addressed to Brian Mulroney, Canada's Prime Minister at the time. The government stated that they received more cards from this initiative than they did for the Goods and Services Tax (GST) vote.

What a phenomenal initiative it was. As Sonia was telling me the story, I was struck by her humbleness. She kept focusing my attention on how saving the jobs of hundreds of people was the most important aspect of what she did. The most significant point in all of this is that Sonia had a belief that this could be done. She didn't assess her ability to make a difference by her position in the company. How could one person so far removed from the boardroom have such an impact? Sonia had a vision, a belief, and a powerful cause. She had a "can-do" attitude. She is a true example of a leader because she ensured that the passion of her vision was more important than the criticism she would receive for her effort. (Many years later, Air Canada bought out Canadian. However, the point of the story remains.)

What are beliefs? Your beliefs are the imprints on your brain that determine the direction you will take in life. Those imprints cause you to see life in a particular way. They are what you base your actions on. Here's a simple example. If you wore rose-coloured glasses, everything would be rose in colour. The metaphor is that you would see only what is good in the world and not what is wrong. However, we need to be able to discern what is good and what is not in order to acknowledge and move toward that which is right and progressive. On the other hand, if you were a chimney sweep in England in the days of the industrial revolution and wore glasses that you never cleaned, you would see a world that was very dull grey or even black. Many people see the world this way too. They have gathered evidence of how bleak life is. The difference between the two outlooks is in our underlying beliefs.

Beliefs shape our actions. If your belief is that the earth is flat, you are unlikely to get on a cruise ship. If you believe that you are unattractive, you may shy away from people. If you believe you are not good at math, you are less likely to become an accountant. If you believe you are a poor speaker, you will avoid speaking in front of people. As well, if you believe you are personable and fun, you are likely to be more gregarious. You have literally hundreds of beliefs both positive and negative. They are what make an individual unique. Beliefs make up your character and your personality.

If you still believe that your teacher or parents are responsible for the lack of success in your corporate climb or your status, this section is for you. During the initial months and years of your life, your personality was formed in two ways. You learned to imitate, and you moved from discomfort to comfort or from pain to pleasure. The most important part of your personality development was how much love you received through touch, facial gesturing, voice, food, etc. The degree to which you did not receive love was the degree to which you felt deficient. With this deficiency you felt like you needed to compensate and you did this by crying, misbehaving, or performing positively. Alongside of this, if your parents made the mistake of demonstrating conditional love, you felt like you had to work even harder to get more love. Conditional love is when a parent or teacher uses love to manipulate behaviour. An example of conditional love is if you ate your food the right way, your parents were really pleased but if you did not they expressed dissatisfaction, irritation, or even anger. You interpreted this as when you did something good you were loved and when you did something bad you were not. We recognise that this is not the goal of the parent. Of course a parent still loves his or her child when the child is doing wrong but this is not what the child perceives. This sets up a belief system that the child always has to do something good in order to get love. Look at yourself and look at other adults. Do you go out of your way to please people to feel valued or loved or do you do things simply out of your own freedom of self-expression? The latter is considered a healthy way to live.

Another negative belief created during childhood is when children are told, "No," "Put that down," "Don't touch that," "You'll hurt yourself," "Get out of there," "You can't do that." After a while, the child internalises these comments as personal failures and begins to be less adventurous and curious. It has been estimated that the average two-year-old receives 432 negative and 32 positive communications in a day. We know that a child would not live past the age of two if parents avoided correction and discipline. It is a necessary part of growing up. However, if the parents do not back up emotionally delivered correction with positive and loving reinforcement, they run the risk of the child interpreting "you can't" into "I can't." The child learns to fear failure and learns to avoid trying new things. This extends right into the school system where teachers and authority figures may have communicated the same way. The child may have developed a belief system where he or she was afraid to try anything new. Studies show that a child's self-esteem is lower at the end of high school than when he or she first enters kindergarten. Do you wonder why?

Destructive criticism also feeds these negative beliefs. If children are constantly told that they are stupid or lazy, that their work isn't good enough, they may fear trying anything new for fear of being criticised. The most insidious problem occurs in the adult years when we cover, defend, and justify the manifestations of our deficiencies. We make statements like, "That's how I am" and "It's their fault."

Another way beliefs are formed is through Critical Incidents (CIs). A CI is an event in a child's life when trauma occurs, and based on the interpretation of the event, the child began to form a positive or negative belief. It is like a record in the brain and memories are the grooves symbolising beliefs. Here is the order in which a CI maps onto the brain:

1. **The experience or incident occurs.**

2. **You perceive it in a particular way.**

3. **The experience, plus an emotion, is logged into your memory.**

4. **If it was strong enough, it begins to form a belief system by mapping other memories supporting the initial belief on top of the previous one. The groove then deepens.**

5. **Simply by rethinking and/or talking about the incident, the belief is strengthened and the groove deepens further.**

Here is an example to which we can all relate. A second-grade teacher has asked the children to share stories about what they did in the summer. Mary gets up to speak, but in the middle of her story the other children burst out in laughter. Mary doesn't know why. At that point, Mary thinks, "Hey, I'm pretty darn funny. I like this standing up and talking. I can make everyone laugh. I'm the centre of attention." Mike gets up to speak and the same kind of event happens, but instead he thinks, "They're all laughing at me. I must have said something stupid. I don't really like this. I'll never speak again!" Mary, for some reason, chooses the positive belief, and Mike chooses the negative. What is going to happen when next Monday the teacher asks the class to talk about what happened on the weekend? Mary is going to retrieve the memory she has of this kind of experience, relive the emotions in her mind and will be relatively excited and confident. She will probably do well at talking again. In her mind, she has a positive association. Now Mike is going to pull out his negative record. He's going to go up there shaking in his sneakers and the kids are going to know it. There is a strong possibility that things won't go well for him again. The current belief gets reinforced and he's off and running to being one of those people who would rather die than speak in public. And here's the tragedy. He may have been one of the greatest speakers to have ever lived. Our mind is like a jukebox full of records, both positive and negative. All day long we pull out and play these records. However, the secret to success is in creating new memories to replace the old ones. We have all had and will continue to have these critical incidents in our lives. But, it is how we learn to communicate with ourselves and interpret these CI's that will make the life-altering differences.

To understand better what happens in the brain, psychologists often divide the human mind into a mind/body model. The model says that you simultaneously live in three distinct planes: You are spiritual (sub-conscious), you have an intellect (conscious), and you live in a physical body (body).

Conscious Mind

This is the part of the body that interacts directly with the world. It thinks, it reasons, and it holds your free will. It is important to understand that your conscious mind can accept ideas, comments, and pictures, or it can reject them. No person or circumstance can cause you to dwell on thoughts you do not choose to think about. That's where you have to be careful. People or circumstances can be a strong determinant in causing you to think and react a particular way, but it is *you* who chooses the reaction. For example, if someone cuts you off on the highway, you might say, "He made me so mad!" A more accurate statement might be, "I choose to feel mad because I believe that person intentionally cut me off to make me angry." The thoughts and reactions you continuously choose determine the results in your life. In fact, they determine 99 percent of the results in your life. That might be a little hard to accept but yes you are responsible for your reactions and subsequent actions for virtually everything that is currently happening in your life. As you choose to accept or create these thoughts, they are impressed upon the second part of the mind/body model, the subconscious.

Subconscious Mind

The subconscious mind is the part of you that knows no limits. It can also be referred to as the spirit. This subconscious part of your mind is formed by thoughts that you consciously choose to accept over and over. For example, if someone says you are really considerate and you accept the thought, it becomes a belief and a part of your subconscious. It becomes a fixed part of your personality. Once this happens, we call it a belief system and it becomes unquestionable. This aspect of the mind is also responsible for the manifestation of habits, those things you do without thinking.

We use the subconscious to store information and experiences. Picture the jukeboxes we spoke of earlier. You make a selection, and the arm goes into the record file and plays the record. You hear the words of that record, visualise a picture, and feel an emotion. You have thousands of records stored inside. In anything you do your conscious mind pulls out a record or a set of records, compares it to the current opportunity or experience, and you then make decisions with your conscious mind. The interesting point is that you don't necessarily think about calling up the record or records, they're just there and you then feel the associated emotion. Have you ever been driving along, a song comes on the radio and you suddenly feel blissful or sad depending on the song? What power a song has over us! It's useful when it's on the positive side, but when negative, it is dispiriting…unless you know how to handle it. This occurs not only with music, but also with sights, smells, people we meet, and virtually all incidents that occur. Are you going to use this knowledge to your advantage, or will you be a victim of it?

The Body

The body is a third part of your being, although the least powerful. The subconscious mind manifests itself through your body via your words, your expression, and the energy you emit. The feelings that come from your self-conscious mind influence your emotions and therefore your body.

I have taken some of my seminar participants to the top of the CN Tower in Toronto, Canada, the world's second tallest free-standing structure. As they travelled up the tower some of them were almost sick from the rapid acceleration of the elevator. On one particular occasion when we arrived at the top, the outside railings had been removed for repair, and we had to stay behind a barrier. There were however temporary ropes strung across where the railings had been removed. I knew the person in charge of construction, so he allowed us to attach ropes to ourselves and reach out to within one foot of the edge. We decided that as a group we would take steps in unison toward the edge of the structure. The cold wind was blowing in our faces. Some of the participants had to stop short for they became fearful. Still others looked over the edge and felt the exhilaration of it all. The significant point here is that while people's emotions were real, their experiences were not. You see, the participants never left their seats. I had taken them through a visualisation exercise. However, most of the participants reported feeling some kind of physical manifestation based on an image in their minds that I helped to create. The participants had previous experiences or records locked in their subconscious minds. Each experience had a physical/emotional attachment that was re-experienced during the visualisation.

We can re-experience pain, love, hate, anger, exhilaration, or any emotion based on what we choose to remember or what image or visualisation we choose to create in our mind. This is both a blessing and a curse. It's a curse when we allow ourselves to bring up hatred or anger while thinking of the past; it is a blessing when we think of good memories or when we choose to change the picture of an old bad memory into a new good one.

Spirit

The most important aspect of your being is spirit, but this is a subject to be researched elsewhere. Yet, I tell you that it is the most important subject that can be researched. When Jesus was talking to his disciples He said, "I go so that the Counsellor can come." I invite you to find out about this, one of the greatest mysteries and gifts that human-kind has ever received.

Expectations Create Reality

We also have beliefs about others and these beliefs can have a strong impact on their lives. A famous study done in a school exemplifies this power of belief. Dr. Robert Rosenthal, a Harvard psychologist, teamed up with a San Francisco school principal named Lenore Jacobson. The purpose of the study was to determine the answer to the question, "Do children perform badly in school because their teachers expect them to?" If this were true, they extrapolated, if they raised the teacher's expectations, then the students' performances would improve. The experiment went as follows:

A group of kindergarten to grade five students was given a learning ability test. In the fall, teachers were given the names of six children who were identified as "spurters" - those with exceptional learning ability. The teachers were reminded to treat these children like the rest of the class. At the end of the year, all the children were tested again. Of course, those who had the high IQs finished at the top of the class just as expected. Here's the catch, and an amazing revelation it is. The children who were identified initially as the top six were merely average students at the beginning of the year. The test results had in fact been rigged. However, the test results at the end of the year were not rigged. They scored far ahead of the other children and had gained 15 to 27 IQ points over the year. Furthermore, the teachers described these students as "happier, more curious, more affectionate than average, having a better chance to succeed at life."

Because the teachers in this experiment had been led to expect more from certain students, the students came to expect more of themselves. The irony is that the most important changes occurred in the attitudes of the teachers. Dr. Rosenthal explained that the teacher's tone of voice, facial expressions, touch and posture stemming from the internal belief of their high expectations was the reason for the remarkable result. The elevated teacher beliefs ignited the intelligence which already existed within the minds of the students.

I personally believe this is one of the most revealing experiments of our time. It verifies the immense power of belief in others, and how it can change lives. Our children, students, friends, employees, bosses—everyone we meet—have both positive and negative, good and bad, ambition and apathy, strengths and weaknesses. As parents, teachers, friends, managers, employees, we can choose daily to concentrate on weaknesses or build the strengths. What an amazing opportunity we have to transform lives simply by knowing and understanding this power of belief and its effect on others.

> *Treat a person as they appear to be and you make them worse, but treat a person as if they already were what they potentially could be, and you make them what they should be.*
>
> **—GOETHE**

I can verify this over and over because I have been a teacher. One example among many that comes to mind was a young grade sixer who was and believed he was a failure at math. He would often affirm his stupidity and would quit before even trying so that his results would line up with his beliefs. Of course he was unable to see it this way at the time. When he would make self-deprecating remarks, I would not allow it and would affirm that he was an intelligent boy. In fact, I would make him say it. Then I would incite him to work hard. He did keep working and over the period of three months he moved from a C- average to a B+. I held the high expectations until he was able to take over on his own based on his results. A new groove was etched in his mind. Good work Andrew!

Rosenthal II

Sometimes a one-time research study is not sufficient to dispel a myth or ignite a belief. Dr. Rosenthal went on to do more experiments. At the beginning of the school year, the principal called three teachers into his office and said, "As a result of your teaching excellence over the last few years, we have come to the conclusion that you are the best teachers in the school. And as a special reward to you, we have identified three classes each with 30 of the brightest students in this school—the students with the highest IQs. We're going to assign them to you to teach for the entire year. Now, we don't want to be accused of discrimination, so it's very important that you do not reveal to these children in any way that you know they've been selected for a screened class. And second of all, we're not going to tell their parents, because we don't want to cause any difficulties there. I expect you to teach exactly the same way you normally do and use exactly the same curriculum, and I expect you to get very good results with these students."

At the end of the school year, these students led not only the school, but also the entire school district in academic accomplishment. Their grade levels were 20 to 30 percent above the grade levels of the entire school. Calling the three teachers into his office, the principal said, "Well, you've had quite a good year."

"Yes we have…it was so easy," replied the teachers. "These children were so easy to teach. They were eager to learn and it was such a pleasure to teach them."

"Well, maybe I better tell you the truth," said the school principal. "This has been an experiment, and those 90 children were chosen out of the school at random. When I assigned them to your class at the beginning of the year, I had no idea what their IQ scores were at all."

"That's incredible!" exclaimed the teachers. "But how could it be that they scored so highly? They did so well. They got such good grades. We can only draw on the conclusion that we are such excellent teachers."

At which point the principal said, "And I think I should also tell you the other side of the experiment. At the beginning of the school year, we put all the teachers' names in a hat, and yours were the first three to be drawn."

Isn't that amazing! Average students plus average teachers combined with high expectations combined to create excellence. You achieve what you expect to achieve and what others expect you to achieve.

To broaden your understanding of beliefs, I have categorised them into two types: personal and universal.

Personal Beliefs

These are beliefs that people *know* are true about themselves. They are locked in ideas about their personality and their capabilities. They are analogous to branded markings on the brain, which seemingly cannot be removed in the mind of the believer. Here are a few examples of negative beliefs:

- I'm not good at math.
- I'm not a good storyteller.
- I'm not good at sports.
- I'm shy.
- My relationship with my parents will never be good.
- I'll never get married.
- I'll never be a good mother.
- I could never be slim.
- Men just don't know how to communicate with me.
- I can't deal with difficult people.
- My child is shy so I better protect him.
- We could never own our own home.
- Getting ahead is too much work.

Later you will see that you are not stuck with your negative beliefs. Here are some examples of positive beliefs:

- I am good at math.
- I'm an "A" student.
- I have great athletic abilities.
- People like me because I have a nice personality.
- I'm fun to be around.
- I'm a dynamic person.
- I'm courageous.
- I always succeed somehow, some way.

- **I am a wonderful mother.**
- **I know how to manage finances.**
- **I believe that love can conquer everything.**
- **There is a God and He is helping me in my life.**
- **I am intelligent and resourceful. I always figure things out.**

Universal Beliefs

Universal beliefs are what we believe about life outside of our personalities. I spoke earlier about the flat earth belief. In fact, in 1491 the earth *was* flat. It was flat because people believed so. Since they believed it was flat, their actions followed suit, and nobody ventured to sail out into the ocean too far until our friend Christopher Columbus made the attempt.

When my Dad was young, he used to read a comic called *Buck Rogers.* Buck used to get into so-called rocket ships and fly off into space. It was absurd. People knew you couldn't fly off into space. I mean, they really knew you couldn't. Now we are sending probes to Mars. Look at how the universal beliefs have been altered. Here are some examples of negative universal beliefs:

- **Generation Xers have much less financial opportunity.**
- **Most businesses fail within three years.**
- **Fifty percent of marriages end in divorce.**
- **The terrible twos.**
- **Teachers are overpaid and are doing a poor job.**
- **All teens are uncommunicative.**

I could never list all of people's beliefs. Only you can list what you know isn't working in your life. Take some time and list three of your own negative universal beliefs.

1. ______________________________

2. ______________________________

3. ______________________________

We live in accordance with our beliefs, however positive or negative, true or false they may be. Most of the time we are completely unaware of those beliefs. When we think about our personality, we accept it as given. We are just as we are. How many times have you heard people say, "That's me," "That's my personality," "That's the way I am," or, "It's not my personality," "It's not my nature?"

In the book, *Developing the Leader Within You,* John Maxwell explains that in 1940 the Swiss employed 80,000 people in the watch-making industry, and 80 percent of the watches sold in the world were from Switzerland. In the late 1950s, digital watch technology was made known to the Swiss, but they rejected the idea because their universal belief was that they *knew* they already had the best watches and the best watchmakers. Today the Swiss employ only 18,000 people, and 80 percent of the world's watches are digital. Holding on to beliefs can be costly.

Understanding your negative personal and universal beliefs is important. When you begin to write your goals, your negative beliefs present themselves. You must be able to recognise them or they will prevent you from succeeding. Instead of believing that you have a negative personality trait for life, know that you can change it. It all starts with recognising and then re-programming.

Chapter 7 — Summary

Don't Believe Your Beliefs

- Remember that if others can do it, so can you.
- Your beliefs are formed from incidents in your life.
- You can start recognising the records or beliefs that you play without knowing it.
- You're not stuck with how you are. You can change if you decide.
- What we believe about others and ourselves become self-fulfilling prophecies.
- Dr. Rosenthal revealed the power of positive expectations. Expect the best around you without judging. Expect the best from yourself.

Stay Fired Up!

8

PROGRAM YOU FOR PROSPERITY

Have you ever thought about another person's success by saying, "Oh, he was born with a silver spoon in his mouth," or "She just has what it takes, that's all!" If you truly believe that those are the reasons why others are more successful than you are, I invite you to reconsider. The reason people are successful is because of how they think. It is the beliefs that have been ingrained in their minds by their parents, teachers, friends and society. It is also because they have learned to formulate positive beliefs and to choose the best for themselves. I love what the former world freestyle-wrestling champion Chris Wilson says at his motivational addresses:

> *We weren't born winners and we weren't born losers, but we were born choosers, and we can choose to be happy.*
>
> **—CHRIS WILSON-FORMER WORLD FREESTYLE WRESTLING CHAMPION**

Chris would know. He chose to set a goal to become the best in the world in his sport. Chris wrote out his goal accompanied by a detailed plan and worked for years to finally accomplish his dream. We *always* have the power to choose. The single most important factor in being successful is this ability to choose. Henry Ford is famous for saying, "Whether you can or whether you cannot, you're right!" If you believe you cannot change your beliefs, you might as well put this book down, for you are admitting that from an intellectual point of view, you have progressed as far as you can go. Although your material life may improve, the excitement of growing will be gone. Remember, if you're not growing, you're dying. When you don't believe you can change, you're giving up everything that could be better in your life. To say that you are now the best you will ever be is self-defeating; it signifies the disbelief in the magnificence of your own existence. You will also be passing on that belief to your children, friends, and colleagues.

A 7 - Point Strategy To Change Your Negative Beliefs

You *can* change your beliefs. You can change how you see the world. You can heal damage that has been done. You can reshape your life, and you can help those around you to do the same. If you and your children for example are currently doing well, you can *ensure* the continued success by being very clear about those beliefs and values you are passing on. You will equip yourself and them with power to fend off the enemies of doubt, peer pressure, fear, and media influence. To change your beliefs for the better, you must start with your mind.

1. Make a decision that you are going to change, and seek all that life has to offer.

This is critical. You must become determined. You cannot say, "Well, I'll see if this is going to work," or "I'll try this," or "This stuff works for some but not for others." This thinking will bring you more of the same results. Remember, if you continue to do what you've always done, you'll continue to get what you've always gotten.

2. Recognise your negative beliefs.

In order to discover what your negative beliefs are, look at your life and ask the following questions. Note that this might be a little confronting but do not be anxious for you are learning new ways to replace poor performance. Is your relationship with your spouse strong, loving, caring, open and intimate? Is your relationship with your children honest and respectful? Is your relationship with your parents caring and loving? Are you financially prosperous? Are you excited about waking up every morning? Is your life a wonderful example to all who see and hear you? Be careful not to start in with excuses, justifications or rationalisations about why things are the way they are. As the author of *Jonathan Livingston Seagull* so cleverly put it:

> *If you argue for your limitations you get to keep them.*
>
> —RICHARD BACH

What about your children's lives? Are your children enjoying studying and are they flourishing in school? Do they have a good circle of friends? Do they discuss their problems with you? Do they complain about everything that happens and blame others? Look also into "key areas" of your life. List some of the beliefs that you feel are impeding your life.

Spiritual

____

____

Health

____

____

Family

____

____

Career

____

____

Wealth

____

____

Friends

____

____

3. Determine Your Positive Beliefs

What *is* working well in your life? Reflect on it and write down your positive beliefs. They might include the following statements. I am a terrific grandmother. I am dedicated. I know how to manage finances. I believe it is better to give than to receive. I have faith that no matter what happens there is a way to solve the problem.

Spiritual

____

____

Health

____

____

Family

____

____

Career

____

____

Wealth

____

____

Friends

____

____

4. Convert Negative Beliefs to Positive Ones

For example, if your old belief system involved the phrase, "We could never afford to buy that," change it to, "We earn the money we need to live the life we choose." I know it seems like a magic trick. It doesn't happen over night, but when you change your belief and start putting that belief into action, things will change for the better. On the opposite side, I can absolutely guarantee you that by continuing with the negative belief you will continue to live out a self-fulfilling prophecy of that belief. Another example might be to change the belief "My spouse is a constant nag." to "My wife cares a great deal about our home and our relationship." If you're thinking, "I'm overweight and out of shape," change it to "I work a little bit each day to reach my ideal goal weight."

Spiritual - New Belief

____

____

Health - New Belief

____

____

Family - New Belief

____

____

Career - New Belief

____

____

Wealth - New Belief

____

____

Friends - New Belief

____

____

Adventure - New Belief

____

____

5. Create Vivid Pictures to Go With the Belief

A picture is worth a thousand words. Be creative. Use the tool of imagination which God gave you to assist in establishing your positive beliefs. For example, if your new belief is, "We earn the kind of money we need to get what we want," you might see yourself writing a cheque for the new boat. If it is, "I always resolve differences with my children," you might see you and your children arguing for a short time, resolving the conflict, hugging each other, and then smiling and laughing. Create the pictures as clear as you can in your mind. Get them as bright as you can and see the details of the pictures in your mind's eye. If you can find actual pictures of your new belief, hang them in your office, on the bathroom mirror, or wherever it is likely to get your periodic attention. For example, if you're trying to become your ideal weight, why not hang a picture of the ideal you on the fridge.

6. Replace Doubts With New Positive Pictures

The moment you acquire a new empowering belief, your old mind-set tries to stop you. The jukebox tries to play the old record. You hear thoughts like, "This is stupid," "You can't be serious," or "You're not smart enough." Fortunately, you have a choice. You must immediately recognise that it is your old conditioning or subconscious talking to you. Immediately say to yourself, "I do not accept that!" or be humorous with yourself and say, "Oh no you don't." and then replace the thought with something positive and useful. Your mind thinks in pictures, so you must immediately replace the negative picture with your new positive image. Do not try to get rid of your old picture or thought first because if you focus on that, it will stay with you. Just insert the new picture and fix your attention on it. Again, make it clear, detailed and bright, and most importantly, put yourself into the picture. Athletes do not succeed if they allow old failures into their mind. They continually create new pictures of their ideal performance.

Another powerful way to influence our belief is through prayer, which is an open conversation with God similar to our conversation with a best friend. God will help you with acquiring material goods as you prove ready to handle them and in matters of forgiveness, family, relationships, and emotional peace, He makes some wonderful promises. I have been assisted many times in my life with prayer both in terms of releasing anxiety and in what I believe to be miracles.

7. Feel the New Emotions

As you continue to employ visualisation to strengthen your personal beliefs, you will become more emotionally involved with the process. Three things will start happening. Number one, you will become more motivated to take action. Number two, your subconscious will be filled with wholesome convictions enabling you to fulfil your goals. Your inner radio tuner will be dialled into the certainty of success. Number three, the results in your life will begin to reinforce those constructive beliefs, and this time the self-fulfilling prophecy will become positive. Remember the jukebox of your mind. You are creating new and positive records.

How can you assist others in developing positive beliefs? Do not allow them to indulge in negativity. Catch them saying negative things and help them change their mind. Catch them doing things right and affirm them. Compliment and admire what they did or said well. Use clear, empowering language. Note when they demonstrate positive beliefs and get them to repeat it.

Remember that what you think about most will occur. You can succumb to negativity by accepting physical, spiritual, and psychological poverty, or you can have faith that you were designed to succeed, to prosper, and to live joyously.

"Happiness is an inside job and you are the sole architect."

MM

Chapter 8 — Summary

Program YOU For Prosperity

- The reason people are successful is because of how they think.
- You were born a chooser. Choose happiness.
- Don't argue for your limitations, argue for the magnificence God intended for you.
- Help others to destroy their negative beliefs while building up positive ones.

Stay Fired Up!

9

BREAK FREE OF F.E.A.R. OF FAILURE

So subtle and deeply seated is the emotion of fear that one may go through life burdened with it, never recognising its presence. Only a courageous analysis will disclose the presence of this universal enemy.

—**NAPOLEON HILL,** *THINK AND GROW RICH*

In the last chapter we discussed negative beliefs. Certainly negative beliefs are very closely tied in with fear. When you learn to recognise fear and worry in your life, you can be set free. Fear and worry are the opposites of truth and faith. These two emotions can slowly erode an individual's early exuberance of youth into a sense of desperation and lost hope. It is fear that breaks up relationships, destroys health, and creates wars. In order to avoid fear and worry, you must learn to understand them.

We have nothing to fear but fear itself!

—**FRANKLIN D. ROOSEVELT**

I used to live in Toronto, Canada in a nice, middle-class area. One summer evening, I decided to stop at a bank machine to get some cash for the next day. There was no one around as I entered the building. I withdrew cash and walked out the front doors with my head down. Suddenly, three men with nylon-distorted faces and waving guns accosted me. It was too bad to be true. I was horrified! The leader grabbed my wallet. As I tried to put up a struggle, he promptly took the back of his gun and cracked me across the side of my head. Adrenaline had overtaken my body and I felt nothing. Their shouting of obscenities rang loudly in the air. They then tried to push me back toward the bank machine to get more money. Apparently I valued my savings more than my life, so I ran. I ran as hard as I could in a zigzag motion hoping to avoid being hit if they fired at me. When I was out of range, I watched them jump into my car and drive away.

That memory is as clear as a bell to this day. And whenever I go to a bank machine, in fact when I get near a bank, without even thinking about it, my hands clench into fists and I instinctively become cautious. I wouldn't call it fear, just a healthy regard for my surroundings. This type of fear is considered healthy. It falls into the same category as walking down a dark alley or driving fast on icy roads. A healthy bit of fear in the right place is a good thing.

What about worrying? Is there such a thing as healthy worrying? The words *anxious, doubtful* and *troubled* are used to define worry. How can one fully engage in life if anxiety and doubt are the predominant conditions of the mind? My friend and mentor Stan Cummings introduced me to this eloquent description of worry by an unknown author:

> *Worry is a thin trickle of fear running through the mind that if unchecked cuts a channel into which all other thoughts are drained.*
>
> —**UNKNOWN**

Worry can also be defined as a sustained form of fear caused by indecision. Some people are so worried about their life that their life passes them by. Earlier in the book you read about the young man who failed out of pilot training due to his fears. You now know that the tragedy could have been avoided. Consider that an acronym for F.E.A.R. could be "Fantasized Experiences Appearing Real." This means that we literally fantasize or visualise a negative picture in our minds and then emotionally it feels like it is real. The more we think about something, the more we turn it into reality.

Before we learn how to overcome fear, let us look at the mechanical aspect of it. When you start thinking, thought impulses immediately begin to translate themselves into action, whether the thoughts are conscious or subconscious, positive or negative. Two thoughts or emotions cannot occupy your mind in the same instant. You cannot be happy and sad at the same moment. You can't jump a skipping rope when you're thinking about getting tangled. You can't love your husband when you keep recalling how he forgot your anniversary. And, you can't land an aircraft when you're thinking about missing the mark. Thankfully, you *can* learn to gain complete control of your thoughts and emotions. At any second, you can choose a different thought. I don't mean that you should turn yourself into a robot. If a special person in your life passed away, it is natural to feel grief. However, if you lose a major account in sales, you can feel glum, disappointed and resentful, or you can choose to feel joyous in the fact that you can learn from the experience.

Most of our human fears are unnecessary. In the book *Think and Grow Rich*, Napoleon Hill analysed the characters of over sixty famous men who had achieved success and were in the top two percent of business. Andrew Carnegie had set Napoleon Hill on this task so that every schoolboy and girl of the day might know the secrets to wealth and success. Carnegie predicted that it would transform the education system if the children were taught these secrets. Six major fears were identified in the study. Those fears are the fear of poverty, the fear of criticism, the fear of ill health, the fear of loss of love, the fear of old age, the fear of death. However, the biggest in the minds of many is the fear of failure.

> *Most people are looking for security and a nice, safe, prosperous future. And there's nothing wrong with that. It's called the American dream. On the other hand, the American nightmare is the FOF (Fear of Failure) complex. Fear of failure brings fear of taking risks… and you're never going to get what you want out of life without taking some risks. Remember that everything worthwhile carries the risk of failure.*
>
> **—LEE IACCOCA (***SAN FRANCISCO EXAMINER,* **JUNE 22, 1986)**

Sometimes in life, it is important to understand what *not* to do in order to know what *to* do. Let us now continue to examine the subject of failure by determining why people fail. The exciting aspect of these reasons is that we have control over them. As you read, assess yourself and use your discoveries in the design of your own success formula.

Lack of Purpose-What is the purpose of your life? You must know your reason for being. You must know why you get up in the morning. If you're not clear about where you're going, how will you know where to go?

Aiming for Mediocrity-When you aim to be mediocre, you quickly outgrow yourself. When you reach a level of competence in your job, your relationship, or even a sport, a malaise sets in. When you are first given any new task or challenge, it's uncomfortable and maybe even painful. But as you work hard to grow and learn to meet the challenge, you feel evolved. I know this was true of my speaking career. I suffered pain through each new challenge, but on the other side of the challenge, I was a more competent speaker, and my character had been strengthened. I could enjoy the fruits of my new ability until the next bigger challenge. Remember that if you aim for the stars and miss, you can still hit the moon.

Lack of Persistence-How many times in our lives have we stopped or quit because we just couldn't find our way to succeed? I remember when I was a young boy I always made the hockey all-star team. When I moved to Ottawa, I did not make the Midget AAA team. I was devastated but still determined to somehow get on that team. I refused to believe anything else.

While playing for my high school team, the AAA coach saw my enthusiasm and budding abilities and brought me back up to his team where I went on to have a great year. The following year I was elected captain. Persistence pays big dividends. We don't know when the breakthroughs will occur. Sometimes it's hours, but other times it's years away. For some, their dream may take a lifetime. The only way to succeed is to never quit.

> *Many of life's failures are people who did not realize how close they were to success when they gave up.*
>
> —**THOMAS EDISON**

> *Never give in, never give in, never, never, never, never - in nothing, great or small, large or petty - never give in except to convictions of honour and good sense.*
>
> —**WINSTON CHURCHILL**

> *Failure is the opportunity to begin again more intelligently.*
>
> —**HENRY FORD**

Indecisiveness

> *Analysis of over 25,000 men and women who had experienced failure verified that the lack of decision-making ability was at the top of the 31 major causes of failure.*
>
> — **NAPOLEON HILL**

When you sit on the fence, you go nowhere. Think about this one. Literally, it is painful to sit on the fence, especially if it's the kind with pointed tops or barbed wire (ouch!). Metaphorically, comfort is on one side and success or failure is on the other. But the middle is the area of pain. People avoid making decisions because they fear making mistakes. But the quicker you make a mistake, the quicker you can learn and then move on to the next decision. Another word we have created for this is *procrastination*. Procrastination is the opposite of decision making. Yet, we make it sound like a valid reason or excuse for our lack of success. "Oh, I've been procrastinating on that," sounds better than, "I haven't had the courage to make a firm decision." I'm not suggesting you just jump in and make decisions irrationally. Seek counsel from wise people, evaluate the pros and the cons, and then decide to act or not to act - but decide!

Poor Self-discipline-There are so many distractions in this world that keep us from doing what we know we must do. I remember that as a kid in high school, I had homework every night. There were always some excellent reasons not to do homework. There were television shows, the ping-pong table, the hockey rink, the phone, chores, watching paint dry, parents to raise—you get the picture. When I showed up the next day without my homework done, I feared and hated the class. When my homework was complete, I looked forward to the class. There's something that happens to us when we invest our time and energy into something. We appreciate it more. We're more committed to it. Even with something as simple as washing your own car, you feel better about driving it once you have invested the energy of fixing it or keeping it clean. All this begins with discipline. Every minute we invest to fulfil our goals is rewarded with a return on the investment, but every minute we waste is gone forever.

Wrong Partner in Marriage-We hear many stories of successful men and women and how their spouses wonderfully supported them. However, a marriage gone badly can take the life out of you.

Marriage can either be heaven or hell on earth.

—ANONYMOUS

One thing that I find paradoxical is that people spend so much time, money, and planning on the wedding, and yet so little on the marriage relationship. We must fend off the negativity and complacency that can creep into our relationships by immersing ourselves in education programs, whether books, courses, counselling, or prayer.

Inability to Take Risks-The inability to take risks is often evidenced by excessive planning, discussion of a possible disaster without presenting solutions, continuing to ask "what if?" questions, and waiting for the "right" time. In my first business, I spent excessive amounts of time doing a business plan and figuring out what my logo should be. What a waste it was. It was only later that I could recognise my fear of risk. Note that I'm not discouraging the creation of a business plan. I am however, calling you to beware that over-planning is a sign of risk avoidance. In order to succeed we must take calculated risks.

Wrong Business Associates-My first business partner did twenty percent of the work, had no investment in the company, and collected fifty percent of the profits. He was shocked when after six months I told him we had to part company. I have also made many mistakes listening to so-called business gurus and their success stories. We must carry out "due diligence" on those with whom we associate. Be careful! It's better to have one reliable ally than ten whose reputations are questionable.

Wrong Vocation-Do the very best you can at whatever you're doing, but if you are dissatisfied with what you do, then have the courage to let someone else do your job and move on. Do it responsibly, but do it. What is the point of investing forty to fifty hours per week if you hate what you do? You won't excel in the way you could have in some other position. Ask yourself if you would discover more success in a job you are more passionate about.

> *Many people work very hard to get to the top of the ladder; the problem is that when they reach the top they find out that it's leaned up against the wrong wall.*
>
> —**DAVE PHILLIPS**

My friend Brent Roberts was an account executive in one of the top five advertising firms in Canada. He chose to leave it because he discovered he had a passion for building homes. Brent went from a posh job with a secure paycheque to sweeping floors as an apprentice builder. He has worked his way up in the company, and is now known in the city of Vancouver for his excellence in high-quality renovations and the building of custom fine homes. All his work must have an end result of being "peach," which is his word for first class. Brent is passionate about what he does. That passion and subsequent happiness spills over into his family and social life. Find out your strengths and what you are passionate about and go after it. Keep working towards doing what you love.

> *Continue to do what you need to do when you need to do it, and a time will come when you can do what you want to do when you want to do it.*
>
> —**ZIG ZIGLAR**

Lack of Concentration-Often we go to work and think about home and then we arrive home to our family or friends and think about work. Flitting around, doing a bit of this and a bit of that dramatically reduces our productivity and sense of accomplishment. We live in a world of comforts and distractions. For example, television or aimless Internet surfing can be alluring devices that keep people from succeeding. We must pick time slots and totally throw ourselves into the task at hand each new day.

> *The measure of a person's success is a function of his or her ability to concentrate on a single thing at a single time.*
>
> —**JIM TALLMAN -TRAINING SPECIALIST**

Poor Money Management-My friend Jeff Gunther, who has been successful with money, was giving a talk on financial success to a group of college and career students at his church. He announced that he would be revealing the "three secrets to financial prosperity." The room was packed on the night of the talk. In a hushed voice, Jeff asked one of the participants to close the back door in order to fully capture this life-altering secret. In a very serious manner, with just a hint of sarcasm, the following secrets to financial success were revealed: (1) earn more money, (2) spend less than you earn, and (3) invest the difference. The crowd looked around waiting for more but was to receive nothing else. You may be waiting too. It's disarmingly simple and yet how many of us do just the opposite? We run up credit by buying things we want but don't need. We stay in dead-end jobs. We don't invest. The irony is that we often complain about our debt load, while sitting in our new car, or on our leather couch, or after we get back from Club Med.

Dishonesty-Recall that one of the criteria for success is peace of mind. How can you have peace of mind if you are constantly on the lookout for fear of being caught in a lie? Dishonesty often starts small - robbing the company for time spent not working, overextending breaks, or going a little over on the budget. The danger is that we justify it by saying we deserve it, or that the company will never miss it. But *we* know it, and it *does* affect us. It is a joy to be able to look people in the eye and know that you are a person of integrity.

Blame-As soon as you blame someone or something you lose your power. How often have we blamed the government, our neighbour, our teacher, our boss, or God? Oftentimes, when you attack and criticise others, you are putting them down to make yourself look better. Try this - point to someone and say, "It's your fault." Look at your hand. Notice that one finger is pointing at them and three are pointing at you. As the Nazarene carpenter says, "Why do you look at the speck of sawdust in your brother's eye and pay no attention to the plank in your own eye?" There is always something *you* can do to make life better.

Association-This is one of the most common reasons for failure. A very good friend of mine was once a top hockey player in the Ontario Junior A Hockey League. He was drafted by a NHL team but became involved in activities that ruined him. By associating with the wrong crowd he began using substances that damaged everything in his life. What a waste of human potential it was! (I am happy to report that he has beaten his addictions is, now a successful business owner, masters in divinity graduate, and part-time pastor.)

Study the following suggestions and adopt the ideas as a part of your success strategy. Given that we have identified the causes of poor success, would it not make sense to do just the opposite?

Lack of a definite purpose

- **Search out and lock in on a definite purpose.**

Aiming for mediocrity

- Aim high. Shoot for the stars!

Lack of persistence

- Keep going. Never quit. Keep striving.

Indecisiveness

- Make up your mind. Decide and get going.

Poor self-discipline

- Do what you know you must do.

Wrong partner in marriage

- Study marriage and relationships prior to getting married. If you're already married, attend education and counselling courses.

Inability to risk

- Take intelligent risks and learn from mistakes.

Wrong business associates

- Choose wisely. Find out their background. Put them through tests. Do your due-diligence and have a personality profile done for each partner you want to work with. Decide if you can agree on values.

Wrong vocation

- Learn where your strengths and interests lie. (I also recommend a personality profile. There are many out there and I am thrilled with the Birkman system which Dave Phillips did for me.)

Lack of concentration

- Focus on a single thing at a single time.

Poor money management

- Earn more money than you spend and invest the difference.

Dishonesty

- Develop integrity. If some mistakes were made in the past, acknowledge them and apologise for them. You will make more mistakes. Keep cleaning them up, asking for forgiveness and moving on.

Blame

- Point the finger at yourself and change your behaviour first. Find out what you can do to remedy the situation.

Poor association

- Find solid, honest, hard-working, joyous people to associate with.

If you are still not motivated to move beyond your fears, allow these famous failures to inspire you. You will see that they did not see failure as such but only as results. With each new result they discovered what did not work, and then kept working until they found what did. (These captions were taken from the book Chicken Soup for the Soul-1st Edition.)

Richard Bach

Twenty months after receiving his wings, Richard Bach resigned from the Air Force. He then became editor of an aviation magazine, which went bankrupt. When he wrote *Jonathan Livingston Seagull,* Bach couldn't think of an ending, and the manuscript lay there for eight years. Eighteen publishers rejected it before the book became a best seller.

> *You only have to do a few things right in your life so long as you don't do too many things wrong.*
>
> —WARREN BUFFET

Diana Ross and The Supremes

In 1962, four women wanted to get into professional singing. They started out by performing in their church. They recorded nine songs which were all failures. The group was nicknamed the No-Hit Supremes. In the summer of 1964, "Where Did Our Love Go?" raced to the top of the charts, and the Supremes became a household name.

Abraham Lincoln

Take a look at the chronology of this former U.S. president:
1816—Family was forced out of home. He worked to support them.

1818—Mother died.

1831—Failed in business.

1832—Ran for state legislature: lost. He lost his job and was rejected from getting into law school.

1833—Borrowed money from a friend to begin a business and by the end of the year was bankrupt. Spent 17 years paying off debt.

1834—Ran for state legislature and won.

1835—Was engaged to be married but his sweetheart died.

1836—Had a total nervous breakdown and was in bed for six months.

1838—Ran to become speaker of state legislature: was defeated.

1840—Ran to become elector: was defeated.

1843—Ran for congress: lost.

1846—Ran for congress-won.

1848—Ran for re-election: lost.

1849—Sought the position of land officer in his home state: lost.

1856—Sought the vice-presidential nomination at party convention and got less than 100 votes. Ran for U.S. Senate: lost.

1861—Elected president of the United States of America.

(Adapted from *Chicken Soup for the Soul.)*

Babe Ruth
Babe Ruth struck out 1,330 times but hit 714 homeruns.

Fred Astaire (very famous dancer and singer)
After Fred Astaire's first screen test, the memo from the testing director of MGM, dated 1933 said, "Can't act! Slightly bald! Can dance a little!" Astaire kept that memo over the fireplace in his Beverly Hills home.

> *I have always felt that although someone may defeat me, and I strike out in a ball game, the pitcher on that particular day was the best player. But I know when I see him again I'm going to be ready for his curve ball. Failure is a part of success. There is no such thing as a bed of roses all your life. But failure will never stand in the way of success if you learn from it.*
>
> —**HANK AARON**

Ludwig van Beethoven
Beethoven handled his violin awkwardly and preferred playing his own compositions, instead of improving his technique. His teacher called him hopeless as a composer.

Sir Winston Churchill
Winston failed sixth grade and didn't become Prime Minister of England until he was 62, after a lifetime of failures.

Thomas Edison
His teachers said he was "too stupid to learn anything."

Albert Einstein
Albert did not speak until he was four and didn't read until he was seven. His teacher described him as "mentally slow and adrift forever in his foolish dreams." He was expelled from Zurich Polytechnic School.

Henry Ford
Henry failed and went broke five times before succeeding.

Richard Hooker
Richard worked for seven years on his war novel *MASH.*

Though 21 publishers rejected it, it went on to be a best-selling book, movie, and television series.

Leo Tolstoy
The author of *War and Peace* flunked out of college and was described as "unable and unwilling" to learn.

> *The way to accelerate your success is to double your failure rate.*
>
> —**TOM WATSON, SR., IBM**

> *Every failure is a stepping stone on the road to success, moving us closer to our desired destination.*
>
> **MM**

Let these people inspire you toward the magnificence inside of you. They all started off just like you and many failed their entire life until they finally achieved greatness. This greatness is attributable to the character they developed through the seeking of wisdom and by perseverance.

Chapter 9 — Summary

Break Free of F.E.A.R. of Failure

- Fear and worry are the opposites of truth and faith.
- Overcoming fear starts with a purpose that you must develop.
- Many great men and women failed but they kept going until they succeeded.
- There should be no such word as failure. There are only results. If they're poor results, then learn and move on. If they're good results, then celebrate.

Stay Fired Up!

PART III

Plan to Succeed

10

DREAM THE POSSIBLE DREAM

Motivation is for those who lack purpose.

—DAVE PHILLIPS

The technology of goal setting and achieving is one of the most important motivational activities for human beings, and yet it is seldom taught. You will minimise a host of problems in your children, your family relationships, your business, and in your health, if you will only learn to understand and practise the art of goal setting.

Why We Absolutely Need Goals

The above quote by Dave Phillips is not to dissuade you from thinking about the subject of motivation but is saying that when you are clear and focused, you don't need to be motivated. That is, you will be inherently motivated by seeking after your goals. Let us illustrate the importance of goal setting using our health as an example. As part of his motivational addresses, Zig Ziglar asks if anyone in the audience has a million-dollar racehorse. Usually nobody raises a hand. He then asks if they did have a million-dollar racehorse, would they keep it up half the night, feed it chips, pop, or alcohol, and not let it get any exercise? "No?" "What about a ten dollar dog? A five-dollar cat? No? What about a billion-dollar body?" Zig is right. We *have* been given billion-dollar bodies that are miraculous beyond our comprehension, and yet we fill them with sugar, white flour, MSG, additives, pop, fats, alcohol, and more. You might want to justify your condition by saying, "I work hard and I deserve a little reward." You're right! Reward yourself by giving your body the best. It is no secret that if you had clear goals for your optimal health, you would be in better shape physically. When you set a goal to reach a certain weight, to exercise a certain way, to feel a certain way, your mind and body go to work to achieve those goals.

If you have tried and failed in the past, it is because you may not have followed a good plan.

The subject of students and homework reveals another example of the value of goal setting. It is easier in the younger grades to get children to do homework. We use parent techniques that range from inspiration to manipulation to threats. But as children progress to where they seek greater autonomy and independence, it can be harder to get them motivated. We tell them to do their homework. They ask why. We say, "So you will pass school." They say, "So what?" You say, "So you can get a good job." In grade seven, getting a job is not a pressing issue. As adults, we *know* they need to do this, so we try to force them by telling children what's good for them without motivating them to do it. Your boss tells you to call a hundred clients asking their response to the question, "Do you take the lint off your old socks or do you buy new ones?" If you asked why, and your boss told you because it's going to be good for the company, you wouldn't be all that inspired to do it, would you? But if she said, "We're producing a new anti-lint sock product and we want to know what people think," you would be more motivated because you would be clearer about the goal. But we don't do that with our children and we often fail to do it with adults and even ourselves. What if your boss said, "For every customer who wants a free sample of this product, you get a dollar bonus," you would be further motivated, wouldn't you? You would take more ownership of the goal. Now the question is, "Do you have goals you're focusing on?"

Goals help us to overcome problems. At the time of writing this book, I was counselling teenagers from various families. Parents typically called me because their children were having trouble in school. Many children were either not interested in school or hated it. The children could not understand the reason for school. Most had some sense that education was a good thing, but the lack of a clear understanding of its purpose provided little or no drive to pursue it. Some children can do well without a goal, while others do better if they have one. They need to see the big picture. They need to understand the purpose of their efforts. This explains why so many children do poorly in school, give their parents grey hairs, and cause their teachers to despair, yet when they get out into the real world they become successful citizens because they find goals they can get excited about. They find a reason for being. But why must children wait until they get out into the real world? Why not teach them to set and achieve goals now? Why not prepare them to be in charge of their own lives?

Many people live their entire lives as followers. They work for the few that *do* have goals. They are "slaves" – paid slaves, but slaves nonetheless. They're unmotivated and uninspired. Do not misunderstand me. Service, whether paid or not, is a noble and essential aspect of living. To serve is a privilege and an honour. But even in service, we need our *own* dreams and goals.

During my counselling sessions, I used to ask young people what their goals were. That question would be enough to awaken the teen's curiosity. My next step in the counselling process was to take them through a process of goal setting. As a result, they would begin to light up. Their problems seemed less important as they became focused on something bigger and brighter. They would feel more in control and without knowing it would begin to take accountability for their own lives. Parents and principals reported back that the child's behaviour had miraculously changed. You see, if you inspire young people, if you get them to focus on their dreams and empower them to take more responsibility, then many of the other problems will take care of themselves. This philosophy also applies to adults!

> *Cherish your dreams and visions, for they are the children of your soul, the blueprints of your ultimate achievements.*
>
> —**NAPOLEON HILL**

Goals help to overcome negativity. When I was substitute teaching, each morning I would get a phone call at 6am telling me what school to go to. On this particular morning, the call was for an alternative school, one that taught students who did not fit in with the regular system. I walked into a class where seven kids were slouched in their chairs. I told them that we were going to do some dreaming and goal setting. They gave me a blank stare as I posed the question, "If you could have anything, and do anything you wanted, what would it be?"

One volunteer looked at his peers, as if summoning their support and answered, "A gorgeous blonde babe, man.... ya, that's what I want." That was a safe bet because his colleagues could approve of that.

"Great," I casually responded. "What else?"

"A 1966 Mustang convertible," he said emphatically.

"Awesome," I said. "What colour? What size engine? How big are the tires? What colour interior?"

His answers came faster, and he looked at his peers less. "Blue, 301, Herst shifter, mag wheels—oversize, white leather interior." As he spoke, I wrote his desires on the board.

"What kind of work do you want to do?"

"I dunno."

"Well if you did know, what would it be?"

He looked at his peers again and responded, "A veterinarian."

His peers burst out laughing.

I wrote "veterinarian" on the board and continued the questioning until a condensed version of his perfect life was on the board. Something came over this young man. Oblivious to his peers' snickering remarks, he became engrossed in something very important – *his life*!

Now, the other students wanted to design their lives too. Unfortunately, the class was over. Would you believe they grumbled about leaving because they didn't have the chance to play the "life design game?" I don't know what became of that young man. I would like to believe that as a result of the short time I spent with him his life changed. On the other hand, I am aware that he had a long history of deep-seated beliefs and habits, which could easily overcome his new dream. Once goals are set, it takes support to carry them out.

When I first started doing motivational seminars for teenagers, a young lady was enrolled in my program. Her mother had brought her for fear of her daughter's future. Part of the workshop involved sharing the intimacies of one's life. As a ninth grader, she told the group stories about her involvement with sex and drugs that made the hairs on the back of my neck stand up. She was constantly fighting with her mother, skipping school, and only God knows what else. The girl was in trouble!

Part of the program was to create a dream chart in which the participants would cut out pictures that related to their dreams and paste them onto cardboard. The philosophy of this is that when you can keep the pictures of what you want in front of you, you are more likely to achieve. Visualisation works in the same way. The program ended and she seemed to leave as a more inspired individual. Her mother called a year later to let me know that her daughter had miraculously accomplished all the goal pictures on her chart. The daughter was even enrolled in a school more suited to her style, and the mother-daughter relationship had improved. Was it the goals that caused the breakthrough in this family? I believe they certainly had a strong influence. The daughter identified what she wanted, and her mother found ways of helping her achieve those desires. The daughter became focused and inspired about life.

The same scenario can occur in the corporate world. Those employees who are involved in the strategic planning for the company and supported in creating goals toward the achievement of the plan are more driven and productive. Does this help the company become more profitable? Absolutely! Reduced absenteeism, reduced attrition, increased morale, and higher customer retention are all results of employee's participation in the strategic planning process. It makes them feel valued and important to the company.

Here is another example of the power of goal setting. Ray Saunders is the man who built the famous Gastown Steam Clock in Vancouver, Canada.

Every hour the clock whistles, and steam gushes out of it. Tourists from around the world come to see it. When I first met Ray, he was one of those geniuses in life who was unclear of his vision. Although he was a successful entrepreneur who had built an excellent business, he had not developed a solid vision and goal plan for his life or business. He was "goal-less." He wanted to engage in some bigger projects with clocks, but seemed unable to break away from the day-to-day operation of his business. Ray completed my Vision to Succeed workshop on goal setting. I then went on to do some consulting for his business and together we designed a strategic plan. He was very excited about it and determined to carry out his plan. One of Ray's key habit changes was to leave the phone answering to his assistant so he could work on bigger projects. I used to call him just to check up and see if he was answering the phone. Eventually, it became harder to contact Ray because he had set up a system to screen calls. My work was done!

A year later, I stopped in to see him. Ray pulled me into his back office and I was amazed. He was totally organised. He had a stunning new brochure of all his projects, a new computer system, his goals clearly outlined, and his mission statement on the wall:

Ray Saunders (Horologist) - Mission Statement

To create public clocks that will, through their sights, sounds and innovative technology, foster civic pride and leave a legacy of usefulness and good feelings for future generations to enjoy.

Doesn't that just make your heart sing? He had developed projects to build clocks around the world and shared with me the work he was doing with a company in Japan. He was more excited about life because he knew what he wanted and was going after it. He had unleashed the genius that was within him. Goal setting and strategic planning really does work. These are but a few examples.

Up to now you have been reading this book in commitment to your family, your business, and yourself. Reading this book is important, but putting the wisdom into action will create a momentum of positive emotions and prosperity that is unstoppable. If you want passion, progress and prosperity, then read on. You've learned about some successes created as a result of goal-setting. Now it's time to understand the strategy of this technology.

Chapter 10 — Summary

Dream the Possible Dream

The following is a list of the benefits you will enjoy if you set goals:

- Awaken each morning with a wonderful sense of purpose.
- Break old bad habits and create new life-giving habits.
- Improve your physical health.
- Overcome depression.
- Increase your self-confidence.
- Improve relationships in your family.
- Improve relationships at work.
- Increase your self-esteem.
- Strengthen your marriage.
- Increase your wealth.

Stay Fired Up!

11

GET STRATEGIC — GET GOING

When Canadian astronaut Robert Thirsk was asked when he first set a goal to become an astronaut, he responded that it was in grade four. As busy adults, we need a system to develop our goals. Setting and achieving goals is a technology, a formula, and a process. When you follow the formula and understand the concepts within the formula, you will achieve more than you've ever dreamed possible. With time, effort, and faith, your goals and dreams *are* absolutely achievable. You will learn to empower yourself and to seek support from a multitude of resources. You will let your self-designed goals lead your life. And the good news is that you don't have to be in grade four. You can be 80 years old and still set exciting goals.

13 Key Elements of Goal Setting

There are thirteen key elements in setting goals, which if followed, will strengthen your chances of succeeding.

1. Goals Must be Based on Your Values

When you are ready to set goals, remember to base them on a sound foundation of values. In my opinion, our values can be thought of in two ways. On one hand, they are what you appreciate and enjoy. For example, you may value spending time with quality people. You may value exercising to keep your body in good physical condition. You may value constant and continuous improvement in your life. On the other hand, values represent the core of your character. They stand for what is important to you. Nowadays, the importance of basic values of right over wrong has been considerably downplayed. We see too many examples of people deciding their next step in life based on their feelings and not on their values. I am not dismissing the value of intuition, but if that intuition is not consistent with a value based on the Judeo-Christian ethic, it is a recipe for trouble. I know that in my life, whenever I pursued goals with questionable values, despite a great effort on my part, there was pain and negative results. An expression we often hear in today's society is, "Oh that's kind of a grey area." What this really means is that the individual is torn between what he wants to do and what he knows is right. He then calls it "grey area." Grey area examples include company expense accounts, falsified tax returns, extra-marital affairs, stealing company time, and empty promises to family members.

The most widely known set of values is found in the Christian faith: honour your father and mother, don't kill anyone, do not commit adultery, do not steal, don't lie, and do not desire other people's possessions. These form the basis of a moral behaviour taught in the Bible. A few other examples of values include:

- **Watch what you say. It can build up or destroy people.**
- **Don't try to give advice to the foolish.**
- **Spend and invest your money wisely.**
- **Be disciplined.**
- **Work hard and your efforts will be rewarded.**
- **Set goals and make plans.**
- **Be cheerful to others.**
- **Don't gossip.**

Did you know that these values also come from the world's best seller in a section called Proverbs which could have also been titled, "Practical Advice for Successful Living." Over and over again the above themes are repeated, along with many others. They are short and to the point. You can read one proverb a day and it will be your guide for living with integrity and joy.

Another kind of value can be found in our "attitude." Here are a few examples of what I believe to be good attitude values, which I strive to live up to, and which you might also choose to commit to:

- **The habit of being happy.**
- **Greet people with enthusiasm, no matter how you feel.**
- **Forgive yourself and be forgiving of others.**
- **Stop yourself from judging others.**
- **Look for the good in all people.**
- **Apologise when you have wronged someone.**
- **Be compassionate.**
- **Have the attitude, "I am responsible."**

- Give to the community.
- Be patient and wait for the right opportunity.
- Turn crisis into opportunity.

Action: Take some time now to write out what values *you* wish to live by.

2. They Must Be Your Own Goals

What in your life are you doing to please someone else? What are you doing in your life in order to fit in? Do you know a Joe who quit his job as soon as his father passed away, or a Jane who became a doctor only because that's what her parents had envisioned for her? Or maybe you chose a university degree when your fondest desire was to become a car mechanic. Your whole life may be set up to please your parents, to be accepted by your friends, or to please society. Ask yourself these questions: Am I working where I want?

Do I have the kind of friends that I truly desire? Am I happy with my state of health? Are my primary relationships blessed? Answer "no" to any of these and you may well be setting goals to please others.

3. Your Goals Must be Created Beyond Your P.E.A.K.

In order to break free of the limiting beliefs about yourself and your life, you must understand that people set limited goals based on their Performance P.E.A.K. - Past, Emotions, Abilities, and Knowledge.

Past—The "P" of P.E.A.K.

When I question people about their goals, they find it very difficult to step outside of what they have experienced. That is, they look at what they have already done and base the next step on that achievement. This appears to be a sound approach. For example, you cannot learn to run before you walk, and you cannot learn to walk before you crawl. If your parents didn't know that human beings were meant to run, they would have not set a goal for you to run. Why? The reason is because a baby is a helpless little person who rolls around in the crib. He tries to stand up over and over but continues to fall. Without knowing that the baby would eventually run, parents would not even try to help him stand up.

Looking at the past in order to set goals limits us. When Roger Bannister broke the four-minute mile, he refused to believe what doctors were telling him – that the goal was impossible, that his lungs would burst. When John F. Kennedy said they would put a man on the moon, he didn't look to the past. If *you* didn't make the hockey or basketball team, don't believe you can't be a champion. If you have had a number of rejections with relationships, don't you dare believe that your life is destined to be lived alone. If you have failed in business, learn from your mistakes and try again more intelligently. You are not your past. You are your potential. The past is only to be learnt from. Don't let a poor past affect how you set goals for the future.

Emotions—The "E" of P.E.A.K.

People often rely on their emotions to make decisions. They let fear get in the way or they feel sad about something, and then mistakenly say their intuition is stopping them. Positive emotions can be wonderful in encouraging you to move forward in life. Negative emotions can also be useful. They may alert you to dangers, either physical or psychological. However, emotions can keep us from our commitments. We may not *feel* like making cold calls, or being nice to our spouse, or jogging early in the morning, so we don't. In the same way, we may not feel like setting a goal or continuing to work on accomplishing it. While I was passionate about using this book to teach others, there were many days when I didn't feel like writing it. But, I learned that my commitments were more important than my emotions. Consider that listening to your emotions can be like asking a toddler for advice. Sometimes we're just not logical with our emotions.

Abilities—The "A" of P.E.A.K.

We all have abilities and lots of them. If you are a secretary in an office, you can type, speak on the phone, manage people, organise files, make decisions, etc. If you work in construction, you can hammer nails, operate eight different pieces of machinery, create concrete forms, order materials, direct cranes, et cetera. If you're in sales, you can make cold calls, develop proposals, do personal sales calls, present your product, do a needs assessment, do follow-up calls, golf (a little humour there for us sales types), and so forth.

When people are looking at new goals they assess their current abilities and decide if they are capable of doing the job or not. An office manager might have an inner desire to manage ten offices across North America, but fears that his abilities are not enough to get him there. They may not be, but in the same way he developed his initial abilities, so too will he learn more. A person selling computers might wish to sell executive aircraft. It may sound too ambitious but he can *develop* the ability to do so and when the commitment is made, he will succeed. Be careful about operating under self-imposed limitations. Where abilities are concerned, you can and will develop them!

Knowledge—The "K" of P.E.A.K.

Another inhibiting factor for setting goals is lack of knowledge. People see a thick manual, or a set of books, or a piece of computer software and think they could never learn "all that." They remind themselves of how much they hated high school or college and relate learning to that. They fear the knowledge. When Henry Ford said he was going to build a V-8 engine, he and his engineers had very little knowledge. They didn't have the technology. Month after month the engineers would say, "Mr. Ford, it's impossible." Each time Mr. Ford would say, "Find a way!" He had the goal, but had to discover the knowledge. When you set goals, don't be limited by your performance P.E.A.K..

The only way to set a goal beyond the P.E.A.K. is to ask the right questions. What kind of a difference do I want to make? What is needed? What inspires me? What would bring others and me more joy and progress? What will I get out of fulfilling the goal? How will it affect my short-term and long-term future? Will it help to create a particular lifestyle? Is this best for my wife or husband? Is this best for my children? Is this beneficial and helpful to society? Is it in line with God's laws of right and wrong?

4. Don't Overset Your Goals, or Set Too Many Goals

Since 1988, I have been an active goal setter. My goal partners and I would meet quarterly to assess, create, and critique our goals. They would point out that my biggest problem was oversetting and creating too many goals. They cautioned me that not achieving my goals too many times could lower my self-esteem. If at the review of your quarterly goal plans, you have achieved only a few, it can create a belief system that you are not very capable when in fact the few goals you achieved can be major accomplishments. But I can pretty well promise you that you will achieve more by over setting than by not setting at all.

5. There Must Be a Strong Reason or "Why?"

If there isn't a strong enough "why" you will abandon the goal when it gets too tough. It is the *why* that drives you. It is the *why* that will carry you through when the chips are down and when you question what you are doing. There has to be a compelling reason that will bring you back to working on the goal. I had several reasons for writing this book. I found that the more I studied human beings, the more I realized how much the society around me was crumbling. I wanted to be out speaking, teaching, and passing on to others what I had learned. As well, people in my seminar programs were asking for it. I had some big whys. There are two major emotions that drive us as human beings, avoiding pain and gaining pleasure. Learning to feel the pain of inaction and visualising the pleasure of accomplishment will help us to amplify the power of why.

6. Take Action

When I first started speaking, I set a goal to speak to a group of a hundred people or more within a three-year period. A few years later I was giving more and more talks to more and more people. One day I was called at the last minute to give a keynote address in place of someone else who had cancelled. I spoke to a crowd of more than a hundred teachers. It was only upon reflection a little later, that I realized, "Hey, my goal has been achieved." I was ecstatic! When you get busy working, your life gets really exciting. Act on your passions daily and some day soon, almost magically, your dreams will come true in ways you cannot even imagine.

7. Identify the Resources That Can Help You

Plans fail for lack of counsel.

—**PROVERBS (THE BIBLE)**

As a child and as a young adult, I wanted to do things on my own. I wanted to show people I could do it. But by not asking for help, I was shooting myself in the foot. I was limping my way to success. If I had learned to ask for help, I would have been years ahead. However, I was more concerned about my ego than fulfilling my dreams and commitments. Getting the credit meant more to me than seeing the results. I have since learned that good leadership is when the job gets done, and the people say, "We did it together." I needed to allow others to make leadership contributions to my causes. We must learn when we set a goal to ask the following questions: Who is an expert at this? Who has done this before? With whom can I partner? Where can I get information on this? Is there an association that can help me? Where else are they doing this? When I engage my audiences in this process with a participant's goal, the number of suggestions and resources from the group is astounding.

8. Set a completion date

You must set a date for the completion of your goals. It changes the goal to a commitment. Typically, we do what is urgent or easy, versus what is most important. With a deadline, you are forced to act. As I was writing this book, I noticed there was always something urgent or necessary to be done. There were days when I promised myself I would write for three hours and before I knew it, two days had gone by without a single word written. Yet I was busy. Can you relate to this?

What is the difference between those who are very successful and those who are not? We all have the same amount of time, twenty-four hours each day. How do some accomplish so much while others do not? Yes, you are busy, but if a goal is something that is truly important to you, you will find a way. You will be forced to be creative, to seek help, to use your resources better. Therefore always set a date.

9. Turn Obstacles Into a Plan

Most of us act negatively toward obstacles. Immediately we think, "Oh no, this is going to be hard!" On the contrary, the obstacles are perfect opportunity providers. They allow you to learn, to grow, to persevere, and to build strength as a person. Get excited about the obstacles. The most exciting aspect of obstacles is that they help you to formulate a plan. Take those obstacles and create ideas of how to overcome them.

10. Create the plan

> *If you fail to plan, you plan to fail.*
>
> —**BRIAN TRACY**

You have to sit down and figure out the details of your goal: How are you going to do it? What are the specific actions you must take? Who are you going to contact? What days/hours of the week will you take to carry out these actions? I know, it sounds like a lot of work, but when you do this, you not only ensure that your goal will be achieved, you also strengthen your commitment and resolve.

11. Your goals must be in writing

When you write down your goal and your goal plan, it forces you to be specific and clear. There is something very different about having a goal in your head versus on paper. It is more believable and more tangible.

12. Visualise your goals

> *Vision provides the destination point of your completed journey.*
>
> —**GREG GERRIE**

Mr. Walt Disney died before Disney World was finished. At the opening celebrations, the master of ceremonies invited his widow up to speak and remarked, "It's too bad Walt couldn't see the completion of his vision." Mrs. Disney walked up to the podium and spoke the following into the microphone, "He did!" and then she sat back down. What a powerful message it was! Walt had seen Disney World long before it had ever been created.

You have to sit down and figure out the details of your goal: How are you going to do it? What are the specific actions you must take? Who are you going to contact? What days/hours of the week will you take to carry out these actions? I know, it sounds like a lot of work, but when you do this, you not only ensure that your goal is going to happen, you also strengthen your commitment and resolve.

13. You must affirm your goals

The power of "right speaking" is so important that I have dedicated a whole chapter to it. For now, start keeping track of all that you say. How many times per day do you speak negatively to yourself and others? How often do you build yourself and others up? How often do you encourage? For now, affirm your goals and speak positively about reaching them.

Climbing On Commitment

In the spring of the year 2001 I wrote a goal to climb Mount Baker in the state of Washington, USA. It was something I had spoken about for years and I was tired of talking about it. I got it into my heart that I was going to do this thing and nothing would stop me. My reasons were that I felt I was slipping. Life had become humdrum. My fitness level had dropped which was an affront to my values. I felt I was becoming complacent and mediocre which was also against my value of growing in all areas of my life. I had stopped growing and when you stop growing you start dying. I needed to achieve something major. To experienced climbers Mount Baker is not a big deal but to me, whose biggest climb had been a three-hour hike, *it was*. Baker, a volcano glacier, was 10,700 feet high. The base was at 4000 feet making the total climb 6,700. I made the commitment to a mountaineering expert and friend and we set a date for the planning meeting.

At the meeting I learned about all the gear I had to obtain. As well, we decided we would do the climb at night when it was colder. This would allow us to walk on hard packed snow. Furthermore, our leader decided we would summit and return to base in one shot. This meant we would be climbing up the glacier for approximately ten hours depending on the weather.

During the next three weeks I began training for the event by doing short hikes, riding my bike, and lifting weights. Compared to the average person, I was in pretty good shape. For a mountain this size, I wasn't so sure. Two days before the climb I pulled a hamstring during a baseball game. I couldn't stop now. I had to do the climb-I had made a commitment to others. I called our leader the day of the climb and we had to make a decision based on weather. There was a fifty-fifty chance of inclement weather, which could result in some compromising conditions. We hummed and hawed but our leader left the decision to me. A feeling came over me and a tiny voice said, "You must do this Greg."

At 11pm that night we began walking. After an hour we hit the snow pack but the grade was fairly easy. Our leader gave me some lessons on the use of the ice pick and ropes in case of a fall. (There were crevasses on the glacier. Some were hundreds of feet down. People had already died on that glacier.) We then attached ourselves together by rope and put on our helmets. I was initially freezing cold but minutes into the next phase was unzipping my jacket. Thankfully, it was a beautiful evening and the stars and partial moon reflecting off of the snow provided just enough light such that we did not have to use our headlamps. As well, an interesting thing happens when you're up high. The light from the sunrise bends around the earth and gives more light to the sky. At 4am, the sky was lit up. It was magical.

The higher I climbed, the more frequent the breaks became. I was amazed at how in-shape my climbing partners were. Kerry, one of the other climbers was a diabetic and her courage and intestinal fortitude amazed me. I on the other hand had not trained long enough and hard enough. By hour seven, I was really hurting. My one leg was weaker than the other and I had to do some compensating. Our leader offered to lighten my pack. I humbly accepted. The time came when we could finally see the summit. The only piece left was called "headwall," the steepest part of the climb. It was about a forty degree angle and was a very long way up.

My only focus was on taking one step at a time. The thin air and the exhaustion made me light-headed. My legs were screaming at me to stop. Every ten minutes I had absolutely nothing left and would drop to my knees and pray, "Please God, help me get to the top." After each prayer my body would go kind of neutral, almost as if the lactic acid was removed from my muscles. I recall doing this six separate times. During this time I also had a vision of my three favourite mentors encouraging me, one from behind and two in front. "Come on Greg, you can do it." It kept me going. Finally at 8:00am we summitted Mount Baker. I was so exhausted that it took me about thirty minutes to start enjoying the beauty of the mountain top. It was a miraculous sight and the view was awesome. I felt like I was in heaven. After four hours walking down, we reached the parking lot. Fourteen hours on the mountain and no sleep - the goal had been achieved. I was both elated and thankful to my climbing encouragers Brian (Mountain Man) Stachniak and Kerry (Never Quit) Cyr.

In analysing the event from a goal perspective, I had done some things right and some things wrong. I set the goal, determined the why, wrote the goal, made the commitment, created a plan, found support, worked hard, utilised my faith, and persevered. My only mistake in the planning was not setting landmark fitness goals to ensure my success. I believe that I received divine help because I can emphatically say I was not in good enough shape to summit. I had however, broken through my self-limitations and this was to be the beginning of the next leg of my life where I was being very challenged in business, finance and relationship. The accomplishment seemed to fuel my passion to succeed at all costs. I knew that if I could do this, I could overcome the other major challenges in my life.

What about you? What is your next summit? Are you backsliding in your life and not maximising your potential? Are you settling for mediocrity when you know deep inside that you were meant for something greater? Now it's time to create your plan.

Chapter 11 — Summary

Get Strategic - Get Going

- Your goals must be based on your values.
- Ensure they are *your* goals.
- Don't use the past to create the future.
- Ask questions that create excitement and challenge.
- See obstacles as a challenge.
- Remember that you are an awesome individual unlike no one else. Maximise your potential.

Stay Fired Up!

12

SEE THE VISION — LOCK ON TARGET

Get excited, it's time to create. This is the chapter you've been waiting for. You've learned about motivation, success, failure, the power of hope, beliefs, self-esteem, and the fear of failure. You've learned the do's and don'ts of goal setting. Now it's time to write. Below is a step by step procedure for setting goals. Follow it, believe it, do it, and you will enjoy the benefits of taking more control of your time and your life. This process will transform your goals from blueprint to reality.

1. Brainstorm

This is how you begin setting goals for your life. Put yourself in a quiet space where you won't be interrupted. Get a pad of paper (or 8 single sheets of paper), your favourite pen or pencil, and a timer of some kind. Dim the lights and sit in your favourite chair. Relax-take a few deep breaths. Smile. At the top of the paper, write the words "Ideal Life." Under ideal life also write the key heading for each page as listed below. Then answer each of the questions associated with each heading. Do not take more than two minutes for each. If negative thoughts come into your mind while you are writing, just ignore them and focus on the question. Write the categories as headings and answer the question for each. Write as much as you can during each two-minute segment. If you stop and take the time to assess your thoughts and ideas, you may begin to doubt yourself. You can have the opportunity to edit your thoughts later. This would also be a good time to pray for guidance. On your mark, get set, go!

Headings

Spiritual-What kind of relationship do you want with your Creator? What truth are you seeking? When you imagine your ideal life, what do you see, feel, and hear? For example, do you feel at peace, enthusiastic, loved, and so forth? What else comes up when you hear "ideal?"(2 minutes)

Health-Describe your ideal health. Think about your body, your appearance, and your mind.

(Remember, no assessing or analysing—it's your *ideal* life.)

(2 minutes)

Mission-If you had all the time, money, skills, and abilities you needed for the rest of your life, what would you do? (This assumes personal cares and worries are eliminated.)

(2 minutes)

Family (parents, siblings, and relatives)

What is perfect "joy" for you when you think about family?

(2 minutes)

If you had all the money and time you needed, what would you do with your family? (2 minutes)

What is "love" to you when you think about family? (2 minutes)

Spouse or Significant Other-Describe what the most wonderful relationship with your spouse, girlfriend, or boyfriend would be like. (2 minutes)

Children-Describe an ideal relationship with your children. Think not of the past but of your ideal life. Be free to dream. (2 minutes)

What I want most for my children is: (2 minutes)

The World-An ideal world for me would be: (2 minutes)

Workplace-My ideal workplace or entrepreneurial pursuit would be and would have: (2 minutes)

TOTAL: 22 MINUTES

Congratulations! You have successfully completed phase I of the goal-setting process. By now you should be excited emotionally, spiritually or psychologically. Put the book down for today and rewrite or type out what you wrote so that it is neat and legible. You can add to the core thoughts, but don't add new ideas. Keep new ideas on a separate sheet of paper. Read your answers again before you go to bed, and in the morning you will wake up with an incredible amount of energy.

By doing this exercise you have ignited a spark within you. On the motivation scale, you can be anywhere from scared to excited. You might be dispirited or disheartened because you have realized how far away you are from your ideal life. You may be electrified or thrilled because you have rekindled some dreams. Wherever you are is absolutely fine.

2. Determine Your Values
Values were discussed earlier. Now is a good time to give thought to them and write them out. Remember that they will grow and change over time, but the core values will remain an important yardstick with which to measure your goals. Please take the time to do this. Goals must be built on your values. Consider writing some core values under the key areas you decide upon as described below.

3. Determine Your Key Areas
Writing goals by "key areas" will help you to cover every aspect of your life. Here is a list of key areas that I teach people to use to set goals: Spiritual, Health, Family, Career, Wealth, and Adventure. However, you may choose your own and call them whatever you want. They must cover all areas of your life so that you can ensure balance.

4. Determine Long-term Goals
Long-term goals are anywhere from three to twenty or more years. The secret of setting long-term goals is not to worry too much about how to reach them. Don't try to figure out how you're going to do it all. Design your long-term goals based on your passions, wishes, and desires from your brainstorm session. Pick one key area and write down a goal. Try to be as specific as possible. Include a completion date and details like colour, size, and so forth.

Examples:

- **I will have my own company providing organic vegetable delivery by January 2007.**
- **I will do my first half marathon by June 2002.**
- **I will have travelled to Nepal by October, 2004.**
- **I will own my own dream home by August 2010.**

5. Determine Why
As discussed before, this is a very important part of goal setting. If you can find big enough "whys," you *will* find a way to achieve your goals. Examples that could apply to some goals are:

- **I love the independence of having my own business.**
- **Remaining fit and achieving big fitness goals inspires me, keeps me in shape and enhances my whole life.**

- **Travel excites me and makes me feel alive and a part of the world.**
- **I want to have a comfortable, secure and enjoyable home to raise my family in.**

6. Determine Yearly Goals
Set your sights on something you can achieve this year.

- **I will work part-time on Saturdays for an organic store.**
- **I will be running 10K by September of this year.**
- **I will have $1000 in the bank by December 25 of this year.**
- **We will put $300 per month in our account each month except December.**

7. Determine Quarterly Goals
Now we're getting closer to home and reality. The closer you get to the present, the more realistic and detailed the goal should be.

- **I will apply for a position in an organic store by Sept 30.**
- **I will run 5 km every second day starting next quarter.**
- **I will create a budget to reduce expenses and increase savings.**
- **I will look for a part-time position to increase cash flow.**

8. Determine Weekly Goals
Weekly goals answer the questions: What will you do this week to help accomplish your quarterly goals? What are your specific targets?

- **I will make two visits to organic stores.**
- **I will run 2 km three times this week.**
- **I will go to a travel agency to research costs.**
- **I will sit down with my spouse to discuss our dream home.**

9. Determine Daily Goals
In your time management system, you should have your top six goals of the day for business and for other key areas.

Examples:

1. **ABC Ltd. appointment.**

2. Complete draft for new marketing idea.
3. Attend noon-hour business Bible study.
4. Make five sales calls. Land one appointment.
5. Study Howard Olsen sales course for 45 minutes.
6. My turn to make dinner. Pick up groceries.
7. Run with my wife at 6:30 a.m.

10. Determine Major Obstacles

Your obstacles become part of the activities for setting your goals. Reflect on the following. What can prevent me from achieving my goal? What do I fear? Once you identify these, they become a part of your plan, which extends from yearly to daily goals.

- **I always break my financial budgets.**
- **I start off strong in my fitness initiatives and then fade off when I get sore.**
- **It all overwhelms me.**

11. Turn Obstacles Into Actions

Here are a few examples:

Obstacle: I always break my financial budgets.

Action: Get accountability coach.

Obstacle: I start off strong in my fitness initiatives and then fade off when I get sore.

Action: Get one or two running partners.

Obstacle: It all overwhelms me.

Action: Read motivational books, listen to tapes, and pray.

12. Determine Resources and Education

Who can help you in your quest? Where are the resources that will teach you? Who can support you?

Examples:

- **Search Internet about the organics industry.**
- **Have a garage sale to get the financial ball rolling.**

- **Find out ways to get cheap mortgages and talk to investment counsellors.**

13. Commit to the Goal

In my seminars, I often ask participants what they feel is the most important reason why people achieve their goals. I get answers such as, writing down your goals, getting help, being diligent, never giving up, visualising, working with the team, and so on. Finally, someone in the group says, "Commitment." Commitment means that you are going to pursue the goal no matter what. You will do everything humanly possible to achieve it. When you say you will be there at 3pm, that's a commitment. When you promise your children you'll be at the school track meet, that's a commitment. You do what it takes to make it happen. The greatest people make commitments and keep them. They find ways to work out the challenges, problems, roadblocks, and feelings. The reason is because they have locked in their mind that they will succeed. They are determined never to surrender. The following is my favourite quote on commitment. Read it aloud with passion and let its words vibrate down to your soul.

Commitment

> *Until one is committed, there is hesitancy, the chance to draw back, always acts of ineffectiveness concerning all acts of initiative and creation. There is one elementary truth, the ignorance of which kills countless ideas and splendid plans: that the moment one definitely commits oneself, then Providence moves too. All sorts of things occur that would never otherwise have occurred. A whole stream of events issues from the decision, reining in one's favour all manner of unforeseen incidents and meetings and material assistance which no man could have dreamed would have come his way.*
>
> *Whatever you can do or dream you can, begin it. Boldness has genius, power and magic!*
>
> —JOHANN WOLFGANG GOETHE

14. Create Positive Habits

There is another key to achieving goals. It is so subtle that people often miss it. It has something to do with your toothbrush. Every morning you get up and brush your teeth. You don't include this procedure in your daily goals. You don't think about the long-term goal of having good teeth at age ninety, then work your goals backwards, down to your yearly goal, then down to a quarterly, weekly, and daily. You don't write on your daily goal list that you must brush your teeth - you just do it without thinking. It is a habitual action, and it keeps your breath fresh and your teeth and gums in good shape. It's the small but important things that we do automatically on a regular basis that advances us towards our goals.

As you work your goals down to their smallest "to-dos," there will be some that you will need to do daily in order to succeed. If you are a teacher, it may be to greet the children joyfully every day. If you are an aircraft mechanic, it may be to ground all engine parts to prevent static charging. If you are in upper management, it may be to walk around the plant at the start of each day, wishing all a good morning. Airline pilots have actual checklists that they go through prior to engine start, after start up, prior to taxi, during taxi, prior to take off, and after take off, until they reach altitude. While there are checklists, there are also habits that keep the aircraft flying and the people safe. We too should have checklists, or what I call, The Habit Keeper, to help us succeed.

After you have completed your goal-setting process for each key area, you will have identified what habits you should be forming. Each day you can look at your chart and check off what you did and did not do. After you get into the habit of doing your habits, you will no longer need the chart. Below is a sample of some habits. Feel free to use them for your own chart.

The "Habit Keeper"

Spiritual

- Read at least one page from a motivational book.
- Read at least one Proverb from the Bible every day.
- Smile and greet people enthusiastically.
- Give thanks for what you have.

Health

- Drink one glass of purified water, first thing in the morning.
- Eat breakfast (fruit and/or porridge with bran).
- Breathe deeply.
- Stand tall. Keep back straight.
- Smile.

Family

- Listen first.

- **At day's end, spend the first ten minutes with family without doing anything else.**
- **Give hugs, even when not in the mood.**
- **Remember the personality type of each family member.**

Career
- **Send sales packages within the hour.**
- **Follow up on hot leads within six minutes.**
- **Return calls in less than eight hours, one hour if in town.**

Wealth
- **Record and tally expenses daily.**

Adventure
- **Plan after-work recreation one week in advance.**
- **Put $5 in vacation jar.**

15. Visualise your goals
A picture is worth a thousand words. It will be advantageous to you if you can find pictures of your ideal dreams and goals. You can make a dream chart out of them or you can carry them in your day timer as I do. When you're feeling unfocused or down, pull out your pictures and gaze at them. Put yourself in the picture. Be there in the middle of your dream. I have both pictures and a schematic of a wonderful dream home I have in mind. I also have pictures of places I want to travel to and some of the toys I would like to have. You must also visualise in your mind what you want. See yourself in the picture. See the colours, hear the sounds, smell the odours. Visualise your dream, or goal, and try to make it as clear as you can in your mind. Allow yourself to smile and become excited. Caution: There are those who think that you can visualise and affirm your way to success. You cannot. Success takes hard work and determination. But these techniques are to help you stay focused and motivated.

Choose another long-term goal from your next key area. Go through the entire process again. Comprehensive goal setting takes time, therefore, make sure that you book time for it in your day-timer. (Goal setting can take anywhere from a half day to two days.) With your first goal, ensure that you take an action … right now. Get going and create some momentum! Here are two more tips on achieving your goals.

Appreciate What You Have - Strive for What You Want

One of the downsides of having a focused vision and an ambitious set of goals is that you might disregard what you *do* have. No matter what your circumstances are, you must adopt an attitude of appreciation. If you live in a shack, appreciate the fact that you have a roof over your head, for there are thousands of people in this world who sleep in the streets. If your job is boring, be thankful you have one. There are millions who are unemployed. If your partner is causing you stress, be thankful that you are not alone because loneliness ages people faster than quarrelling. If you are complaining about not feeling well, think about those who are sick in hospitals or living with serious illnesses. When I get a letter from my World Vision child, who is thankful for the new bench in his school, I feel ashamed. Then I thank God for showing me how blessed I really am.

On the other hand, I also believe it is wrong to accept things as they are if you know they can be better and your quality of life can improve. The key is to appreciate what you have and strive for what you want. Now there's a formula for success!

Choose another long-term goal from your next key area. Go through the entire process again. Comprehensive goal setting takes time, therefore, make sure that you book time for it in your day-timer. (Goal setting can take anywhere from a half day to two days.) With your first goal, ensure that you take an action ... right now. Get going and create some momentum!

Have a Servant's Heart

One of Zig Ziglar's credos is: *You can have everything you want in life if you will just help enough other people get what they want.* When you wake up in the morning ready to help your family have the best day they can, you will be making an excellent contribution. When you go to work thinking that you're going to do all you can to help your fellow employees and to make your customer's day, you're going to have fun at work. If you're not overly excited about your job, but you go in with an attitude to serve and make it the best for everyone else, you cannot help but find your job to be more pleasant. And, eventually you *will* be recognised and promoted, or you will develop competencies to do better elsewhere.

Service is significant because it makes you forget about yourself. Being too self-absorbed may amplify the feelings of self-pity and melancholy. We were made to serve. The sooner you realize this, the sooner you're going to enjoy life to the fullest. That may seem contradictory to the very nature of goal setting, but it isn't really. If your goal is to become CEO of a corporation and earn 200,000 dollars per year, then go for it. On top of that, think how remarkable it will be if in the design of your goal you would wish to make the organisation the most "people caring" organisation in the world. Do you think you're going to enjoy the rewards of your success more? Unquestionably! How different the world would be if we could all focus more on serving each other.

> *Those who will truly be happy are those who have sought and found a way to serve.*
>
> —**ALBERT SCHWEITZER**

Please take the time to sit down and finish your goals. When you do this, you will be on the road to becoming more of a force in your own life and a better contributor to your family and society. You will be in control, excited and fired up!

Chapter 12 — Summary

See the Vision - Lock on Target

- Ensure that values are at the foundation of your goals.
- Develop your goals backwards from far out in the future down to a daily habit.
- The most important aspect of goal setting is making a commitment, preferably to someone.
- While you're working on your goals remember to appreciate what you *do* have today.
- Remember that true happiness is closely tied in with serving others.

Stay Fired Up!

PART IV

Communicate with Power

13

SPEAK WITH POWER AND PURPOSE

> *You cannot rise above what you allow yourself to think or say.*
>
> —**FRANCIS P. MARTIN**

This is one of the most important chapters in the book. It is about the immense power of your words and the effect they have, not only on your life, but also on the lives of others. With your words, you can shatter a heart or build a bridge of understanding. You can encourage greatness or incite rebellion. With your words, you can embrace and love, or reject and despise.

I once heard it said that if we spoke to our friends the way we speak to ourselves, we wouldn't have any friends. Most people don't believe that speaking negatively to themselves would have a negative effect on their life. Look at this example. You may be considering doing your taxes, but make a decision to put it off based on how much effort you know it will take. Upon being asked why you are not in action, you might say, "I'm too lazy." As soon as you say that, it immediately sets up a reaction in your mind that sends you in the opposite direction of your goal. As you verbally reinforce your thought, your imagination takes hold, and it becomes a stronghold, or reality. You *do* become lazy. If others reinforce the fact that you are lazy, it deepens the belief further.

> *Thoughts turn into imagination and imagination is the stronghold of your life.*
>
> —**FRANCIS P. MARTIN**

I once tutored a ninth-grade math student. As I began working with her, her language revealed that she held her math abilities in very low regard. She was convinced that she would never ever become good at it. As I broke down the math into small simple steps, she would continue to say, "I'm so confused. I just don't get it," or "I'm not good at math." Instead of talking about math, I spent time talking to her about beliefs and where they come from. She began to understand that her beliefs and her speaking were the problem, not her intellect. Of course, once she replaced the old beliefs with the new positive ones, her mind was freed up and she started doing very well. I made her affirm out loud, "I am working hard to become good at math." How many students do we have in the world who are doing poorly simply because of their inferior personal beliefs? How many adults have reached their false plateau because they stopped believing in themselves?

Do you control your thoughts? Know that before any word is spoken a thought is created. It is important to know that we *can* control our thoughts. Being aware of this will allow you to edit, accept, or reject them. Where do these thoughts come from? Earlier, we learned that thoughts and ideas continuously accepted by our conscious mind eventually become beliefs and values. In a computer, we can just go in and erase files we don't like by selecting them and hitting "delete." Wouldn't it be wonderful to be able to do the same in our subconscious? Brain scientist Dr. Carolyn Leaf has proven that the negative beliefs in your brain which actually occupy real estate in your brain can be removed permanently. How can you overcome those negative files or thoughts that cause you to speak, act, and experience results in a certain way? You must develop new thoughts that are joyous, prosperous, productive, and constructive to take the place of the old ones.

When the thought "I'm lazy" comes forth, you need to be ready. You need to be armed with the belief that you have the choice to accept or reject the thought. You need to be so clear about who you are that you knock down that negative thought each time, until eventually the new belief system called, "I am a successful, disciplined individual who gets the job done." replaces it. Therefore, technique number one is: Use affirmations to override the negative thoughts that arise. The more affirmations you have in your arsenal, the better it will be for your self-esteem. Here are some examples of positive affirmations:

- **I am alive and exuberant with abundant energy.**
- **I stand tall and happy and ready to succeed in the world.**
- **I am loveable and loving.**
- **I tell the truth all the time.**
- **God only makes winners and I am one of them.**
- **I am organised, intelligent, responsible, and focused.**
- **I am enthusiastic, passionate, compassionate, and positive no matter how bad things get.**
- **I greet people enthusiastically and believe in their magnificence.**

- **I am a winner and today I will win.**
- **I exchange short-term fun for long-term gain.**

If you develop and say these affirmations long enough with passion and emotion, you will believe and adopt them, and they will become a part of you. When the negative or doubtful thought comes into your mind, you will be able to replace it with your high-powered affirmations. Consider that you are literally fighting a battle between the negative and positive side of life. Note that your affirmations should have a strong emotional component in them because words that are not emphatic do not influence the subconscious mind. The principle of autosuggestion is based on this. As part of my affirmation exercise, I memorize Bible scripture. One of my favourites is:

> *Whatever is true, whatever is noble, whatever is right, whatever is pure, whatever is lovely, whatever is admirable—if anything is excellent or praiseworthy, think about such things.*
>
> —**PHILIPPIANS 4:8-THE BIBLE**

Cognitive Dissonance

In music, the word dissonance means disharmonious notes. The same lack of harmony can occur in your conscious mind when you try to implant new thoughts. This disharmony is called cognitive dissonance. There will be a disharmony between the new positive and exciting dreams, goals and affirmations, and your old reality. For example, you may create a picture of you and your happy family, and then a former acrimonious relationship enters the picture in your mind. Or you may see yourself hitting the winning serve in the tennis tournament, and then somehow you double fault in your mind. Do not be discouraged if negative emotions and thoughts try to hold back the new ones. Keep going! Studies have shown that it takes 21 days to develop a habit. Caution: Do not for a moment believe that you can think, visualise, and suggest your way to success. Hard work and continual action are paramount, however, **you must think right in order to act right.**

There are in fact techniques to erase or disrupt those old bad memories. The techniques are found in the study called Neuro Linguistic Programming (NLP). They were first written about by Richard Bandler and John Grinder and made popular by speaker Tony Robbins. Until you choose to research NLP, keep up with your affirmations. To not do this is to miss out on transforming your mind for the better.

Jack Canfield, America's leading expert on self-esteem, suggests that you get rid of negative thoughts by saying in your mind "cancel, cancel." You simply do not let the thought in. If another comes in, say, "cancel, cancel" again, or repeat one of your positive affirmations. When I am attacked by negative thoughts, I say, "thank you" in my mind in kind of a humorous tone, then follow it with an affirmation I know to be true about myself, or by the affirmation of a new belief system which I'm trying to create.

If the negative thoughts keep coming, I resort to prayer. I ask God to take the thoughts away and to grant me peace. Consider that praying is a form of affirmation. You are affirming to God that you have goals for the protection of your family, the success of your business, and for excellent health. As you pray, you also remind yourself and affirm in your own mind what you are seeking.

In the process of communicating there are thoughts that come from listening to others. You can let them in, choose to ignore them, or you can verbalise that you're not going to accept that comment. For example, if a colleague says, "People in government are all corrupt," you can say something like, "I know we have seen a lot of evidence of corruption in our government, but there are plenty of people who really do care about the country." There is responsibility and honour in that manner of speaking. People may reject you for being positive and for holding them accountable for their words. You may lose some friends, but those you do keep will respect you. Another technique that is amazingly simple yet powerful is to say nothing. Walk away saying your affirmations to yourself.

Have you ever spoken negatively about someone? Probably. It was certainly a part of your youth culture and perhaps is a part of your adult culture too. We sometimes derive satisfaction speaking negatively about someone else. Gossip is incredibly destructive. It damages organisations and individuals, but most of all it damages you! When you negatively affirm someone *you* actually feel negative as well. Notice how you feel the next time you "slam," or as our younger generation says "dis" (disrespect) someone.

Gossip: The Silent Killer

My name is Gossip. I have no respect for justice.
I maim without killing. I break hearts and ruin lives.
I am cunning and malicious and gather strength with age.
The more I am quoted, the more I am believed.
I flourish at every level of society. My victims are helpless.
They cannot protect themselves against me because I have no face.
To track me down is impossible. The harder you try, the more elusive I become.
I am nobody's friend. Once I tarnish a reputation, it is never the same.
I topple governments, wreck marriages, and ruin careers,
cause sleepless nights, and indigestion. I spawn suspicion and generate grief.
I make innocent people cry in their pillows.
Even my name Gosssssssssssssip hisses…
I make headlines and headaches.

Before you repeat a story, ask you yourself,
Is it true? Is it fair? Is it necessary?
If not-Kindly STOP! Please !!!
—Author Unknown

The above poem is so very true. Most of us have at one time or another been the victim of gossip. All we can do to prevent it is to ensure that we are not doing the same. And, if you do find someone who is gossiping about you, sit down with them not in anger but in love and find out why they're doing it. Fear not – by being loving and compassionate, they will feel very guilty about what they have done and said, even if some of it was true.

To be a world class communicator, we must choose our words very carefully. Do you ever catch yourself as these kinds of comments slip out of your mouth?

- **You'll never amount to anything.**
- **You're getting fat.**
- **You're incompetent.**
- **The person before you did it better.**
- **Why can't you be like her?**
- **Maybe you should just forget the whole thing.**
- **You call yourself a man?**
- **You're a terrible communicator.**

Surely, there will be times when you slip and blurt out something negative or hurtful. It's never too late to apologise. It takes a big person to say, "That was a thoughtless remark and I am very sorry I said it. Please forgive me." In everything you say, let your words bring encouragement and joy to others.

> *No matter how busy you are, you must take time to make the other person feel important.*
>
> **—MARY KAY ASH**

How often have you said something mean and then followed up with "Just kidding"? For example, you say, "You really are bad at this game.... Just kidding." By that time it's too late. It's like spilling ketchup on someone accidentally on purpose and then telling them you'll clean it up with your wonder soap. There is going to be a stain left. So is it with your negative comments. You're either planting and nourishing positive seeds, or you're poisoning and preventing growth.

Sarcasm is another destroyer of positive attitudes. Sarcasm is calling someone who is overweight "slim," someone who is bald "curly," and so forth. It is a mocking remark. Sarcasm comes from the Greek word *sarkasmos,* which means, "to tear flesh like dogs."

I remember doing a seminar for a group of teachers. I spoke to them about the negative effects of sarcasm, and one of the leaders of the group said in a kind of macho voice that this is how they develop and keep collegiality. One of the group members later confided in me that some of the sarcasm was hurtful. I know it to be true with most people. With every sarcastic remark, amongst all the laughter, there is a piece of one's heart that is "flesh torn." It is much more fun to build people up. Do this at every available opportunity. I was very sarcastic for years until I learned about the damage I was causing. I started changing and made a real effort to edify others. Edify means to build up. I found that I was liked more and as well I liked me more. Try it!

Words produce faith, either good or bad.

—**FRANCIS P. MARTIN**

How would your life change if you set up a filter accepting only what was quoted earlier? Whatever is true, whatever is honourable, whatever is right, whatever is pure, whatever is lovely, whatever is of good repute, whatever is excellent or worthy of praise, think on these things. What if your mind were programmed to use only those categories while speaking? How would your family change? How would your workplace transform?

Man does not live by bread alone. They need buttering up once in a while.

—**ROBERT HENRY, HUMOURIST**

The story is told of a newspaper cartoonist that amused himself one summer day by sending telegrams to twenty acquaintances selected at random. Each message contained only one word, "Congratulations." As far as he knew, not one of them had done anything in particular for which to be congratulated. However, each one took the message as a matter of fact and wrote him a letter of thanks. Everyone who received the message had done something that they regarded as clever and worthy of a compliment. Everyone everywhere is waiting for encouraging words.

There are two things people want more than sex and money, recognition and praise.

—**MARY KAY ASH**

Ascriptive Versus Prescriptive Criticism

Occasionally, there are times when we are called to remark on someone's poor performance either as a friend, a parent, or a manager. There are two ways to do it. One is through *Ascriptive* language, meaning "belonging to," which strongly connects the person to the fault. The other one is *Prescriptive*, which means, "to give direction" and disassociates the fault from the person while letting one know what to do. Here are examples of both:

Ascriptive	**Prescriptive**
You're a bad boy.	Behave yourself.
You're a liar.	Tell the truth.
You're not as smart as Jan.	Jan is a good role model.
You're lazy at your post.	Work hard to meet the requirements.
You're really arrogant.	Be more concerned for others.

Psychologists have found that young children are deeply influenced by ascriptive language in a negative way. They begin to believe that they *are* the fault.

> *Let no corrupt communication proceed out of your mouth, but that which is good, to the use of edifying, that it may minister grace to the hearer.*
>
> —EPHESIANS 4:29 (THE BIBLE)

Apologise

To err is human. We all make mistakes. There have been and will be times when you let your tongue get out of control. You will speak through your negative emotions instead of your values or heart. In such cases, as soon as you realize it, ask for forgiveness and try to repair the damage. If you do not apologize to people, they will hold you in contempt. They may smile at you sweetly but deep down inside they secretly have a dislike and maybe even a hatred towards you. By keeping the following in mind you will increase your chances of saying the right thing at the right time:

> *There are multiple descriptions of the same real world situation. The only justification for language is to empower yourself and others. If the verbal description you create of the situation you find yourself in leads you to a situation of paralysis and ineffectual behaviour, then throw those words away and find yourself a new set. There is always some useful description of the world that*

> *empowers and gives you choices, and your task, if you are going to use words at all, is to find that set of words.*
>
> —**MOSHE FELDENKRAIS**

Remember the immense power of your words and the effect they have, not only on your life, but also on the lives of others. As said earlier, you can shatter a heart or build a bridge. Why not spend the rest of your incredible life building bridges.

Chapter 13 — Summary

Speak With Power and Purpose

- To rid yourself of negative thoughts, replace them with positive affirmations.
- Cognitive dissonance will try to stop the new positivity. Keep striving.
- Try the "cancel cancel" method.
- Pray to get rid of bad thoughts.
- Refuse negativity from others.
- Avoid gossip.
- Stop being sarcastic and start edifying.
- Use prescriptive over ascriptive.
- You can apologise for something you said and ask forgiveness.
- Speak positively or be quiet.

Stay Fired Up!

14

CREATE SUPERIOR HUMAN RELATIONSHIPS

I once had a very poor relationship with my younger sister. I loved her as a sister but didn't like or respect her as a person. As a result of that I spoke to her condescendingly and often doubted her words and actions. But there was to come a day when that would change. The change occurred after I attended an intensive communications program. So powerful was the program that the following weekend, I drove three hours to visit her to discuss our relationship. I took my sister for a walk down an old country road late one Saturday afternoon. It was a warm sunny day and nature was out in all its glory. There was a hill in the distance and we climbed it to enjoy the view and find some solitude. As the sun set in beautiful reds and oranges, I revealed my emotions, frustrations, and sorrows about our relationship. Rhonda couldn't believe her ears.

I apologised to my sister for being arrogant toward her for most of my life. I apologised for all my sarcastic remarks, for the support I had not given her as an older brother. I apologised for my mean spirit and for thinking the worst of her. I expressed my sorrow that we had missed out on being a brother and a sister who loved and supported each other. With tears in my eyes and a choked up throat, I could barely get the words out: "I love you, Rhonda, and I'm sorry I've been such a rotten brother. Please forgive me."

Then the most amazing thing happened. She seemed to drop all her defences. She told me that she didn't hate me as I had thought. I was surprised to discover that she adored me and respected me and had done so all her life. It didn't make sense to me. I was the brother who would mock her, criticise her, and make fun of her. That day, she explained to me that the reason for her overbearing behaviour over the years was because she felt judged and unloved by her family. In a desperate cry for recognition and acknowledgement, she became very demanding. She told me that since childhood her self-esteem was near rock bottom, and she was desperately trying to become recognised as a successful person. On that day, in the span of three hours, we rekindled our love for each other. It was the most amazing scene, and it all occurred because I had been awakened to a new possibility in human relationships.

This chapter contains ideas on how to build superior human relationships. Know that you may have to alter your ways, but be steadfast and you will delight in the magic of being with other people. Follow the principles and you will enjoy a richness and quality in your interactions with others. Here are eighteen ideas to help you grow:

1. Get people out of the box

Growth in our relationships starts with a willingness to allow people to be free of their box. It starts with letting go of our own arrogance in assuming that we know how people are. It's about being open to wisdom versus protecting ourselves from change and growth. The problem between my sister and me was that I didn't *think* she was a particular way, I *knew* it! And I was committed to keep her that way without even realising it. What about you? Do you know how your parents are, how your spouse and children are, how your boss is? The first principle of having superior human relationships is to make a commitment to get people out of the box. You must choose to look beyond their seemingly negative personalities and see the potential of a wonderful person.

2. Acknowledge others

The deepest craving of human nature is the need to feel appreciated.

—**WILLIAM JAMES**

My personal view is that everyone wants to make a positive difference of some kind, no matter how small or large. It could be submitting an idea, changing a diaper in a day-care centre, or running a multimillion-dollar corporation. Did you know that a major reason people leave organisations is because they aren't recognised and acknowledged for the work they do?

I once did a customer service program at a golf course and in a team building session the dishwasher expressed the fact that why should he be involved, he was just the dishwasher. Well I sure did go after him in hurry. I had him see that one spot on a glass, one piece of food particle on a plate, one water-stained piece of silver could undermine all that the restaurant was trying to do to treat the customers first class. He had a real change in heart after that and as well, others saw how important his job was and acknowledged him for it.

Financial reward will only keep people for so long. If they aren't appreciated for what they do, they leave, or they allow "burnout" to set in. We must learn to acknowledge and recognise others for their good performance. We must catch them doing things right.

3. Understand obnoxious people ... and like them

The truth about "obnoxious" people is that their overbearing behaviour hides their true character. They are using an offensive demeanour to cover up a personality weakness. For example, an employee may exhibit haughty behaviour when in effect he is trying to protect himself from criticism. A wise person will always try to find the underlying causes of "difficult" behaviour and by so doing will build good relationships. Thanks to my teaching experience, I have discovered something about people that helps me understand them better: The reason why someone's behaviour is troublesome is likely because in some way, they are hurting inside. A content and well functioning person will seldom find ways to hurt or inconvenience another person. We must recognise this and help people overcome their adversity. We must have compassion for people and be ever cautious of judging them. I know it can be hard...but we must!

4. Build people up and you shall be built up

Studies have shown that when you put someone down, you literally get a chemical transfer in your system that causes you to feel badly, thereby bringing down your own self-esteem. Fortunately, the opposite is also true. When you build someone up, you feel better about yourself. It seems that you were designed to build up and edify others. I encourage you to observe your reactions and feelings the next time that you slander someone. Don't forget to do the same when you praise and support somebody. It's truly amazing!

5. Shake hands, smile and say their name

When you greet someone, do you give them a handshake, a big smile, and say their name? How do you feel when someone does the same to you? It makes you feel important and valued, doesn't it? It is a demonstration somebody is glad to see you. If you adopt this good habit, it will help you when *you* are not feeling great. By focusing on others, you forget about your own problems. In addition, the positivity which you spread around will return to you manifold.

6. Hug people

I've heard many times that in order for us to feel loved and cared for, we need seven hugs a day. There's nothing like a big, friendly "bear hug," or a long caring embrace. Hugs are the exclamation points of body language. They communicate that we are loved and appreciated. Feel free to use them in your physical vocabulary.

Caution: You might want to reserve your hugs for those whom you know well or are intimate with. Otherwise, you may be misunderstood.

7. Give simple words of encouragement

Words of encouragement go a long way to enrich relationships. I have been blessed in my life with many friends who provide continuous encouragement by calling, faxing, emailing or meeting with me. Some of the favourite things they have said to me are:

> *No matter what you do in your life I will always support you and love you.*
>
> **—GORDON GERRIE (MY DAD)**

> *You're a gift to the world and we just have to figure out how to unwrap you.*
>
> **—DAVE PHILLIPS**

> *You are contagiously enthusiastic!*
>
> **—DAVID BENTALL**

> *You're simply world class.*
>
> **—VALERIE CADE LEE**

When I hear words like these, they give me a boost every time. And, when my friends and family need to tell me things that aren't so positive, I am better able to hear them because they have invested time building me up. Doing this for each other is another way of ensuring superior relationships. I too find great pleasure in providing emotional support and encouragement to those around me. Focus on one person today and build them up. Don't flatter them but merely point out what you see them doing well. If they become uncomfortable, recognise that they have a self-esteem challenge. Rest assured that you will have had an impact on them though.

8. Express your friendship with actions

I can think of one friend in particular who encourages me with his actions. My friend Glen Kent has a gift of making people feel special with his words but also with his deeds. He takes the time to think about what others really need in their life and takes action accordingly. If you want superior relationships, doing nice things for others is a great idea. Perhaps you could cut their grass, baby-sit their children, or just take them out for a coffee. The key is to look and see what would make their day. Remember that you will usually benefit more than they will, simply from the joy of giving. Giving is more blessed than receiving.

9. Catch people doing things right

Do you occasionally spot flaws in others? Usually, the better we know a person, the easier it is to notice his or her imperfections. The secret to building healthy relationships, however, is in trying to find out what people are doing right instead of wrong. In so doing, keep in mind that different people have different strengths. What is effortless for you might be very challenging for someone else. For example, speaking in front of people is as natural for me as breathing, yet for others the fear of public speaking surpasses the fear of death. You might acknowledge someone for making an announcement at a meeting knowing their fear of speaking. As a good friend, spouse, parent or boss, seek out the opportunities to acknowledge, praise, and reward the striving efforts of others, no matter how small they may seem to you.

10. Be open and honest

As a management consultant, I am hired to engage a company in Needs Analyses to determine more effective ways to run the company or communicate. Upon investigation with employee groups, I discover that typically there is a lack of openness in the relationship between employees and their managers. Employees are afraid to speak with their managers, for fear of criticism or dismissal. Companies like General Electric have realized this communication handicap and have created a culture where it is admirable to give and receive constructive criticism. Are you one who invites others to give you guidance and correction or are you protective of your own ego in order to avoid a comment which may point out a flaw or weakness?

11. Manage expectations

The reason why people become disappointed and upset is because they have an expectation which remained unfulfilled. They expected you to bring flowers, be on time, respond a certain way, etc, but for various reasons it didn't happen. You're going to disappoint people all your life. Not because you intended it but because you missed meeting their expectations. When that happens, try to find out what that expectation was. Thus, you will be better able to repair the damage and handle future situations. Also know that an upset may not necessarily be about what happened at that moment. When a friend "blows a valve" over a minor incident, know that there could have been other incidents that happened that day, week, year, or even life. Learn to look for what is behind the distress.

12. Be aware of negative anchors

If negative communication occurs between two people enough times in a particular location, negative anchors can be set up. For example, if the dinner table is used as a place to discipline children, or to discuss the negative aspects of the workday, the dining room can become a negative anchor. Your family can feel uncomfortable as soon as they sit down there. A song can also be an anchor, either positive or negative. If the song reminds you of good times, it can put you in a good mood and vice versa. Smells can do the same. Therefore if a friend doesn't wish to meet in a particular location, there may be a good reason. It can have to do with an anchor they don't even understand. Know that it is also possible to create new positive anchors. For example, you might want to make a rule that you only speak positively at the dinner table.

Understand if people are auditory, kinaesthetic, or visual

Another way to understand people and thus create superior human relations is to find out how people communicate. Some people are visual. They need to see pictures of things to understand. They will even say things like, "I see what you mean." If they're auditory, they will like to listen to what you have to say and if they're kinaesthetic, they will want to feel or touch. This has an important bearing on relationships in all settings. Watch, listen and feel for what type of a person your friend, colleague, boss, child, or spouse is. They will connect with you more because they'll sense that you understand and communicate with them on their level. Quite simply, you will be speaking their language. Caution: Placing your hand on the shoulder of a kinaesthetic person may work well but may have the opposite effect for a visual person.

14. Understand the 5 love languages

There is a program called *Love Languages for Couples* developed by Gary Chapman. Its purpose is to help couples identify how they like to give and receive love. The categories are: Encouraging Words, Acts of Service, Gift Giving, Quality Time, and Physical Closeness. To know that your wife's number one language is Acts of Service, for example, is significant. If you, as a husband, are instead, always trying to hug your wife (Physical Touch), or give her flowers (Gift Giving), you're not going to speak her language, and from her point of view you're not going to be demonstrating your love.

One day my friend Greg Pennoyer and I found ourselves painting sixty wide steps leading down to Dave Phillip's house on the water. Dave's wife was currently away on a trip. In the middle of the job, Dave informed us that his wife's number one love language was Acts of Service. My friend and I eyed each other with a wry smile and together we asked, "What's *your* number one language, Dave?" "Physical Touch and Closeness," was the response. We both laughed and continued painting because we knew that Kathy was going to arrive home feeling very loved. We wondered if Dave was living in hope that his expression of love would be matched by what his wife knew to be his love language. All kidding aside, can you see how knowing your mate's love language would be beneficial?

15. Listen, listen, listen

How do you feel when people listen to you? You feel validated, acknowledged, and worthy. When you really listen to someone, they feel like they count. Oftentimes in communication, people have two modes, speaking and waiting to speak. They don't *really* listen. Yet, how good it is to be heard! How great it is when people look into your eyes and nod their heads in understanding. We men have a tendency to look for ways to solve the problem and immediately start providing alternatives. If a person wants your specific help, they will specifically ask for it. Half the time, you will discover that they will solve their problems for themselves during the conversation. By talking it out they will have found clarity in the problem. That is what will help to build their confidence and their character. As a bonus to you, they will walk away thinking what a great conversationalist you are.

16. Love unconditionally and forgive

There are two qualities that are paramount to having superior human relations. They surpass all the techniques, all the right words you say, and all the great things you do. These qualities are *unconditional love and continual forgiveness.* To love someone unconditionally is one of the most challenging things we can do. This is so because we each have our own way of viewing the world. We each have our own beliefs and ideals and they will never be exactly the same as anyone else's. As adaptable as we are, deep down inside we expect others to be like us and to conform to our way of thinking. We don't *think* our way is the right way, we *know* it. There is a definition of love that comes from the Bible that is second to none:

> *Love is patient, love is kind.*
> *It does not envy, it does not boast.*
> *It is not proud, nor rude. It is not self-seeking.*
> *It is not easily angered; it keeps no record of wrongs.*
> *Love does not delight in wrongdoing but rejoices with truth.*
> *It always protects, always trusts, always hopes and always perseveres.*
>
> **—I CORINTHIANS 13 (THE BIBLE)**

Can you imagine if we all conducted our relationships using those guidelines, both in our personal and professional lives? Look at the line "keeps no record of wrongs." This line is about forgiveness. How difficult it is to forgive when someone has wronged us. But not to forgive is to damage ourselves. You don't have to hang out with those who have let you down.

You don't have to agree with what they did or said, but you must forgive them. Forgiveness will restore your heart. Anyone in your life whom you have not forgiven is keeping you in chains and only you have the key to unlock them. How liberating forgiveness is when we finally do it. Who will you forgive today?

17. Appreciate people for who they are
Carl Rogers so eloquently captured the essence of what I wanted to say here that I simply quoted him.

> *I have come to think that one of the most satisfying experiences I know and also one of the most growth- promoting experiences for the other person is just fully to appreciate this individual in the same way that I appreciate a sunset. People are just as wonderful as sunsets if I can let them be. In fact, perhaps the reason we can truly appreciate a sunset is that we cannot control it. When I look at a sunset as I did the other evening, I don't find myself saying "soften the orange a little on the right hand corner, and put a bit more purple along the base, and use a little more pink in the cloud colour." I don't do that. I do not try to control a sunset. I watch it with awe as it unfolds. I like myself best when I can experience my staff member, my son, my daughter, my wife, my grandchildren, in this same way, appreciate the unfolding of life.*
>
> —**CARL R. ROGERS,** *ON BECOMING A PERSON*

Please take the time to appreciate people for who they are now in the journey of life.

18. Risk love
Having superior human relationships is about risking love. How dangerous it is to really love someone! When you love, you're giving away your heart and you can be absolutely sure that someone will step on it, or tear it apart, subtly or brutally. You *will* be hurt. You will have to grieve and take time to recover. But how much will you lose by not loving? To live is to love. C.S. Lewis said it best with this very famous quote on risking love:

> *To love is to be vulnerable. Love anything and your heart will be wrung and possibly broken. If you want to make sure of keeping it intact, you must give your heart to no one, not even an animal. Wrap it carefully around with hobbies and little luxuries; avoid all entanglements; lock it up safe in the casket or coffin of your*

> *selfishness. The only place outside of heaven where you can be perfectly safe from all other dangers of love, is hell.*
>
> —**C. S. LEWIS,** *THE FOUR LOVES*

If you want superior human relationships, you are going to have to be steadfast, change some of your ways, and swallow your ego. You're going to have to give up being right and be the one who takes the initiative when others will not. You will constantly be thinking, "Why am I always the one to have to initiate an apology or a change?" By doing this you are exhibiting the traits of a leader. By doing this you *will* enjoy a richness and quality in your interactions that will bring joy to your own life as well as to the lives of friends, family and colleagues.

Chapter 14 — Summary

Create Superior Human Relationships

- Get people out of the box.
- Acknowledge others.
- Understand obnoxious people ... and like them.
- Build people up and you shall be built up.
- Shake hands, smile and say their name.
- Hug people.
- Give simple words of encouragement.
- Express your friendship with actions.
- Catch people doing things right.
- Be open and honest.
- Manage expectations.
- Understand the negative anchors.
- Understand if people are auditory, kinaesthetic, or visual.
- Understand the 5 Love Languages.
- Love unconditionally and forgive.
- Appreciate people for who they are.
- Risk love.

Stay Fired Up!

PART V

Personal Management

15

KEEP YOUR BODY FIRED UP

When I started my second business, I was so enthusiastic that I would easily work twelve to sixteen hours on many days. I was the accountant, marketer, sales person, motivator, researcher, and presenter. After a year, my friends began noticing that their invitations were always declined. I had become detached and had lost touch with what was important. There was no balance in my life but this remained oblivious to me. In the spring of that year the crisis hit; I was barely able to work a two-hour day and had become somewhat "unglued." It was difficult coping beyond the crisis of running out of coffee. I would wake up tired, unmotivated, and ineffective. I knew that work was necessary, but I just didn't seem to care. Then I felt the guilt set in as a result of my indifference. I think you may know what I mean. I was on the verge of a nervous breakdown and needed a long rest, physically and psychologically.

Today's society has given this stressed out condition a name - chronic fatigue syndrome. It is classified as a disease. I truly believe that at the root of this condition lies poor personal management. I was fortunate to get through a high stress period unharmed, but others aren't so lucky.

Some of the signs of stress include sleeplessness, anxiety, headaches, stomach problems, intestinal problems, and depression, to name a few. What happens physiologically when we undergo stress? A sophisticated group of chemicals is released in the body where a number of neurohormonal changes happen. The brain produces a corticotrophin releasing factor, the purpose of which is to arouse the central nervous system. The pituitary gland releases multiple hormones, the adrenal glands excrete the hormone cortisol, and the brain releases natural painkillers like endorphins. As a result of these releases, we become more alert and more oxygen and sugar goes to the blood, brain, and muscles. It's a miraculous chain of events that occurs almost instantly. The bad news is that if the events that cause the stress are allowed to continue indefinitely, problems will occur. If not resolved, multiple disorders may begin to manifest in the body including tissue ageing and immune system malfunction. In the long term, this may lead to infection, cancer, stroke, and other maladies.

We have seen that the world is in crisis everywhere. Dr. Richard Swanson best explains these crises in his book *Margin*. He points out that we have crises in the following areas: crime, drug-abuse, national debt, health care, sexually transmitted diseases, adolescent suicide, environmental, divorce, teenage pregnancy, pornography, inner city war zones, single motherhood, litigation and liability, and employment. This has been amplified by the power of media. Each day we experience war, famine, violence and murder in our own living room. Watching and reading the news is like drinking orange juice concentrate without the water—it's just too rich. The acid from the juice burns as it goes down the throat and then it sits in the stomach and eats away at the lining of the stomach.

Continually being exposed to negativity without the proper balance of living purposeful lives has us run the risk of developing a feeling of hopelessness. As a result, we become afraid, insecure, nervous, and strung out. It eats away at the core of our psyche. Perhaps this explains why we see so many more cases of stress-related diseases. Just look at the word "dis-ease." It means "not at ease." I'm not suggesting that we overlook all the bad in the world and just focus on the good, but we must keep our own life positive and in balance in order to ward off stress.

Modern civilisation has also added to our health problems. We are inundated by the modern phone, including features like call waiting, allowing us to become more stressed by talking to two people at once. So many conveniences designed to create productivity have also created more stress. As well, we have more competition, more information to process, and more decisions to make. A single edition of the New York Times contains more information than a 17th century British subject would encounter in a lifetime. Harvard economist Juliet Schor explains that the average American will work the equivalent of one month longer this year than 20 years ago. *The amount of leisure time enjoyed by the average American has decreased 37 percent since 1973. The average workweek has gone from under 40 hours per week (including commuting) to 47 hours per week.* (Nancy Gibbs, "How America Has Run Out of Time," *Time Magazine*, 24 April 1989)

Various studies have shown that husbands and wives spend less than fifteen minutes of quality time per day relating to each other as a married couple in love. It all adds up to more stress. All these interruptions, information, and work overload have cost us a lower quality of living and premature ageing.

According to gerontologists, the following are factors that contribute to stress and ageing. Measure yourself against this research:

- **Lack of regular routine _____**

- Lack of regular work schedule _____
- Job dissatisfaction _____
- Can't express emotions _____
- Feeling helpless to change self _____
- Living alone _____
- Absence of close friends _____
- Forty-plus-hour work weeks _____
- Financial burdens _____
- Habitual or excessive worry _____
- Regret about the past _____
- Critical of self and others _____

Did you know that fear and worry cause stress and ageing? When you look at the problems of your life, it's not the creditors that are going to kill you, it's the worrying about them that will. It's not the loss of your job that is causing you damage, it's the worrying about it. It's the FEAR (Fantasized Experience Appearing Real) that we spoke of earlier. In another chapter, I spoke about the visualisation of a group going up the CN Tower. The candidates actually felt afraid and had the physical manifestations of nausea simply by thinking about looking over the edge of the tower. Extensive research has shown that when you imagine it, from a stress point of view, you also experience it. When a stress is remembered or visualised, the same set of destructive hormones is released as if the individual were actually experiencing the stress itself.

In Deepak Chopra's book, *Ageless Body, Timeless Mind*, his thesis is that ageing can be prevented or at least slowed down. He reveals some fascinating research, proving that one's state of mind has a powerful effect on stress: Recent widows are twice as likely to develop breast cancer. Chronically depressed people are four times more likely to get sick. Breast cancer spread fastest among women who had repressed personalities, felt hopeless, and were unable to express anger, fear, and other negative emotions. (Note that I am not in agreement with all of Mr. Chopra's philosophies. He had completed some excellent research that I wanted to quote.)

We *can* slow down and apparently reverse the premature ageing process by controlling our minds and our environments. In 1979, a group of psychologists led by Dr. Ellen Langer took a group of men who were 75 years and older to a country resort for a week. (Some of these men were dependent on family members to perform everyday tasks.) The entire resort was set up as if it were in 1959, including reading materials and furniture. The men were asked to act as they would have twenty years earlier. This included discussions about how things were going in their careers and how their wives and children were doing. The men were spoken to by staff as if they had all the abilities and mental faculties of a younger group. They also wore ID photos from 20 years earlier. The results of the study were remarkable. Compared to a control group, who also went on the same retreat but without the twenty year reversion strategies, these men were more active and self-sufficient at mealtime, were more independent in room clean-up, exhibited lengthening fingers (opposite of ageing), had more flexible joints, had better posture, had stronger hand grip, and improved hearing and had improved vision. Over half of the group had their IQs return to 1950 levels. (Deepak Chopra-Ageless Body, Timeless Mind)

As you see, by acting as if they were younger and by being treated younger, the minds of these men caused a physiological shift. Their ageing reversed. What are the implications of this? You be your own judge. I *do* know that when I'm in the right state of mind, I feel like a teenager. This study gives us some very strong evidence about the power of the mind to combat stress and consequently ageing.

Now that we have a fairly good idea of some of the causes of stress, let's look at sixteen ideas to help you live a life that's more fun and less stressful.

Manage your thoughts. You have a choice of what to think about. Each time you receive a negative thought, you can accept or deny it. If you choose to accept it, it is added to your subconscious mind and becomes reality to you. Therefore think positively.

Take the "I am responsible" approach. One of the challenges in experiencing adversity is the feeling that you are out of control. It is a helpless feeling for most human beings, however, it is not hopeless. How can one regain control of their life, or situation? In an earlier chapter, I spoke about the power of affirmation. Here is another one. Think of an area in your life where you feel out of control, stressed, or unhappy. You sense that there's definitely something wrong but you don't know what to do. Now say the following with real conviction and strong emotion:

I am responsible!

I am responsible!

I am responsible!

Notice the feeling you get. There is a powerful psychological transformation that occurs. The power starts to come back to you. You stop blaming others, life, destiny or God. You begin to focus on what *can* be done. You may choose to work through it and know that your character is being built. You may choose to have a chat with your boss or to quit the team, but you have taken back responsibility. You have chosen to take control and make the most of a negative or perplexing situation.

Make happiness a habit. You *can* make happiness a habit. You can get up in the morning and choose to be happy. In fact, in nearly *all* things we can choose to be happy. Go ahead-say it, "I choose to be happy!" Now be it!

Plan your time for work and recreation. The next chapter is devoted to time management, but for now, know that if you plan your time you *will* have more control. If you have more control, you *will* feel less stressed. If you do not plan for free time, then work and other people's agendas will use up that time. Remember to book time and do some fun recreational things.

Express your emotions. Some people are more reserved than others are. Regardless, if you keep all your negative emotions inside, you are going to build up resentment and anger, which will progressively eat away at you. You may eventually have a nervous breakdown or become ill. If you know you have trouble expressing your emotions, get help. My mother is one of the nicest people I know. For the first half of her life, she allowed others to sometimes mistreat her while she remained silent. She categorised this as "being nice." I remember it used to really bother her. She has since learned to be more expressive and to reveal her emotions. She says what's on her mind, and the bonus is that people now respect her for her endearing personality and her willingness to stand up for herself. She has learned that while confronting a situation may initially create conflict, the matter can be settled without harbouring internal resentments.

Crying can be another way of expressing your emotions. The research is still ongoing, but it has been discovered that one of the many chemicals released in tears is called leucine-enkephalin. This chemical is classified as an endorphin, which is one of the body's natural painkillers. There's something about subduing pain that is associated with crying.

Use adversity to build character. When you're under stress and suffering, you can choose to see it as building your character. As you experience the tough times, keep in mind that what doesn't kill you can only make you stronger. You are being annealed like a sword in the fire. You are building resiliency, mental endurance, and an ability to find joy in the worst of times.

Focus on one day at a time. Many of us are worried about the future. We're concerned about keeping our job, the safety of our kids, our finances, or even tomorrow's weather. Decide what your primary concerns are and make a plan of action to address them. Do not waste your time with idle conversation surrounding all your anxieties. You're just stirring up more negativity. Take your goals and make them into a daily plan. Decide what you're going to do today and focus on it. My older sister continuously reminds me to take it one day at a time.

> *Who of you by worrying can add a single day to his life?*
>
> **JESUS CHRIST**

Focus on others. University of California psychologist Larry Scherwitz taped the conversations of 600 men, two thirds of whom were healthy, while the other third had heart disease. In listening to the tapes, Dr. Scherwitz counted how many times the men used the personal pronoun "I" and "me" and the possessive pronoun "mine." He found that there was a direct correlation between the number of times these words were said by the participants and the state of their health. In further studies, he found that the more an individual talked about himself or herself, the greater the chance that he or she would have a heart attack. How much do we focus on our own material wealth, security, time, and fun? How much do we give up for others? How much do we sacrifice our own needs to make someone else's life better? **It seems that having a heart for others produces in you a better heart.**

> *Make a difference! You have to be here anyway.*
>
> **—DAVE PHILLIPS**

A professor at a college once gave an assignment to his students. It was to go out and perform a kind act outside of the classroom and then come back and report the results. Ironically, the students reported that *they* got more out of doing the deed than their beneficiaries received. You may have heard of the book *Random Acts of Kindness*. It is as a result of the professor's study. The students found more joy in helping others and of course, joy can relieve stress pretty quickly.

> *The greatest pleasure I know is to do a good action by stealth and have it found out by accident.*
>
> **—THE ATHENEUM, 1834**

Eat and drink for health. Many of us have allowed ourselves to adopt a lifestyle that promotes convenience over health. We eat highly processed foods, drink too much coffee, and consume too much fat. Before we know it, we're overweight, our heart doesn't work properly, we can't keep up with our children, and we run the risk of dying prematurely. How can we really expect to keep up our strength, our health, and our motivation, if we're not giving our bodies the proper fuel it needs? Here are nine simple tips that will help you stay physically healthier and Fired Up for Life!

- Drink a glass of purified water when you get up in the morning (your body is dehydrated). You should drink seven more glasses throughout the day.
- For breakfast, have some fruit and/or a bowl of real, not highly processed, porridge and a glass of juice. Studies show that those who eat breakfast live longer.
- Eat plenty of fruits and vegetables. When cooking vegetables, steam them for a short time because the longer you cook them, the more you destroy important enzymes and nutrients. Consider buying a juicer.
- Consider taking mineral supplements. Our soils have been depleted of many minerals that we would normally get in plants that utilise the soil.
- Buy organic foods. You can get anywhere from five to forty-five times the value in terms of nutrition. (I recognise that this can be expensive. Perhaps grow your own vegetables.)
- Go easy on dairy and meat products, which can clog your system.
- Do not eat heavy meals any later than 7 P.M.
- Limit yourself to a maximum of a glass of wine over dinner or one beer per day.

None of these suggestions are difficult to follow. Keep asking yourself, "Am I worth it?" Of course you are. Make these changes today and get some people to support you.

Take supplements. Author Robert Allen in his paper, *Your Health Today* (1998), gathered extensive research material that highlighted the origins and nature of disease in today's world. Most of the statistics below came from that paper which referenced 116 research studies, books, and other sources. The paper attributes a dramatic increase in disease to the foods we eat. There has been a rampant increase in what he calls the Deadly Seven: heart disease, cancer, stroke, diabetes, arthritis, osteoporosis, and Alzheimer's. Listen to these statistics: Cancer is up 44 percent since 1950. Breast cancer is up 60 percent and prostate cancer 100 percent since 1950. According to the *Journal of the American Medical Association,* one in every three adults has heart disease, including hardening and clogging of the arteries. The incidence of diabetes has risen over 600 percent in little more than one generation. 80 percent of Americans develop some degree of arthritis by age 60. Only 20 percent of cancer is hereditary; 80 percent is within your control.

This article and many other studies confirm that our chemically saturated soils have prevented plants from getting the normal soil nutrients, which we used to get. Consequently, we have deficiencies in our diets creating the increase in these diseases. To add to this, we use more pesticides and nutrient destroying preservative processes, which further deplete the system.

Here are some interesting facts about vitamins as contained in the study mentioned above: You have to eat 75 bowls of spinach to replace a bowl of spinach you ate in 1948. According to one UCLA study, only 300 mg of vitamin C per day can add six years to your life. People who have taken 400 IU of vitamin E per day, for at least ten years, lowered their risk of heart attack by 90 percent. High vitamin E has been shown to reduce colon cancer by 68 percent and also reduces cataracts by 56 percent. According to a study by Dr. Larry Clark of the University of Arizona, 200 mcg per day of selenium will cut prostate cancer by 69 percent, colorectal cancer by 64 percent and lung cancer by 34 percent. Dr. Ananda Prasad, M.D., Professor of Medicine at Wayne State University School of Medicine did a study and discovered that subjects who took 30 mg of zinc gluconate every day for six months saw their immune functioning come dramatically alive. 85 percent of men with enlarged prostates can find relief with adequate intakes of zinc. When given B12 supplements 20 to 30 percent of Alzheimer's and dementia-diagnosed patients were cured.

I hope I've made my point clear in that you should be either eating an abundance of fruit and vegetables, organically grown if possible, or taking supplements. If you can, it is wise to do both. But before you proceed with the supplements, most definitely consult with the right doctor.

Exercise your body. Our bodies, unlike machines, get better with use. Well-exercised leg muscles do not deteriorate with time - they get stronger. As well, the leg bone mass gets stronger in proportion to how much weight is put on them. Furthermore, ligaments, which hold the knee together, get thicker and strengthen with more exercise. At Tufts Ageing Centre, it was discovered that runners' forearms had a higher bone density than those of non-runners. It appears as if a signal is sent to the entire body to increase calcium everywhere when you exercise.

People who exercise generally have fewer illnesses than those who do not. Exercise stimulates the nervous system enabling us to cope with stress. It reduces osteoporosis and obesity, improves blood flow, and reduces depression. Dr. Steven Blair at the Institute for Aerobics followed a group of 13,000 men and women and found out that those who followed sedentary lifestyles had mortality rates three to five times higher than those who exercised. The good news is that you don't have to be a fitness fanatic to receive benefits. A thirty-minute brisk walk every day is reported to have the same anti-ageing benefits as running thirty to forty miles per week. Exercise is known to create a host of other benefits, but the sum total of them is reduced stress and longer life. Would you make a commitment right now to begin an exercise program, even if you can only manage a one-minute walk down the block in the beginning? It's a start. Get going now!

Work on having a happy marriage. Do everything you can to have a happy marriage by reading, listening to tapes, going to seminars, and asking for help from others and the good Lord. Learn to communicate with your spouse. Love him or her unconditionally; attend special events designed for couples, grow in knowing each other better, and make it a habit to work on your relationship continuously.

Create a satisfying career. Learn to do the very best you can in your job. If you are dissatisfied, then work toward a higher position in the company or find a new position in another company. It will only harm you and the company to be disgruntled.

Excel at managing your finances. Since finances can be a major source of stress, learn to take control of them. Develop a savings plan. Create and follow a budget. If you're not earning enough, find ways to earn more. Realize the difference between what you *want* and what you *need*.

***You* control the technology in your life**. Be conscious of your pager, cell phone, email, and Internet. Don't surf the Internet without a specific agenda. Always ask if the search is helping you in your primary directive. Decide when it is important to use your pager. Tell your company that you wish to have specific times available with your friends or family, then shut it off and leave it at home. Resist the temptation to check messages when you're taking time off. If you carry a cell phone to stay in touch with personal friends and family and you get a business call during personal time, say, "I would love to speak with you, but I need to call you on Monday morning." Make a mental or written note of it and keep playing. Even better, have a different communication system for work and personal life.

Reflect and Journal. Taking the time to reflect on your day will also give you a sense of control. Discuss with your partner or friend what you learned, the mistakes you made, and the victories you accomplished. Write them down and you will discover the benefits. **Be thankful for all the blessings in your life.**

Practice these health ideals and you will release the incredible energy potential that is within you. Keep the right fuel in you and you will be Fired Up For Life.

Chapter 15 — Summary

Keep Your Body Fired Up

- Manage your thoughts.
- Take the "I am responsible" approach.
- Make happiness a habit.
- Plan your time for work and recreation.
- Express your emotions.
- Use adversity to build character.
- Focus on one day at a time.
- Focus on others.
- Eat and drink for health.
- Take supplements.
- Exercise your body.
- Work on having a happy marriage.
- Create a satisfying career.
- Excel at managing your finances.
- You control technology in your life.
- Reflect and journal.

Stay Fired Up!

16

HAVE THE TIME OF YOUR LIFE

The clock of life is wound but once, and no one has the power,

To tell just when the hands will stop, at late or early hour.

Now is the only time you own; live, love, toil with a will.

Place no faith in tomorrow for, the clock may then be still.

AUTHOR UNKNOWN

As success-oriented individuals, we must ask ourselves what the cost of poor time management is. Do any of the following apply to you? You're flying out the door in the morning and halfway to work you remember you forgot something important. At the end of the day, you feel you didn't get anything major accomplished. Others seem to get more done than you do. You keep rewriting your to-do lists and the same things are being rewritten. You notice your relationship is slipping. You apologise a great deal. You're often late. You just don't seem to have peace and joy in your life.

By managing your time well you will be able to make the most of the time given to you and overcome many of the problems stated above. The following strategies and techniques will help you have "the time of your life."

Take care of the big rocks first. An expert in time management was speaking to a group of business students. "Okay, time for a quiz," he said and pulled out a one-gallon, wide-mouthed mason jar which he set on the table in front of him. He also brought out many fist-sized rocks and carefully placed them one at a time into the jar. When the jar was filled to the top and no more rocks could fit inside, he asked, "Is this jar full?" Everyone affirmed that it was full. The time management expert questioned, "Really?" He then pulled out a bucket of gravel, poured it in and shook the mason jar causing pieces of gravel to work themselves down into the spaces between the big rocks. He then asked the group once more, "Is the jar full?" But this time the class was on to him. "Probably not," one of them answered. "Good!" the expert replied. He reached under the table and brought out a bucket of sand and proceeded to pour the sand in the jar. It went into the spaces between the rocks and the gravel. Once more he asked the question, "Is the jar full?" "No!" the class shouted. A pitcher of water was then poured in until the jar was filled to the brim.

Then he looked at the class and asked, "What is the point of this illustration?" One of the students raised his hand and said, "The point is, no matter how full your schedule is, if you work really hard, you can always find time to do more." "No," the speaker replied, "that's not the point. The truth this illustration teaches is if you don't put the big rocks in first, you'll never get them in at all.

What are the big rocks in *your* life? Is it time with your loved ones, your faith, a worthy cause, or mentoring others? Perhaps making sales calls first thing in the morning is your big rock. Maybe buying your wedding anniversary gift *today* is big. Finishing the dry walling could be the big rock, or so could attending your daughter's grade two play.

Here is a good method for establishing your priorities:

1. **List the 15 most important things you do in your life, in no particular order. Do this by thinking through your day, from the time you get up to the time you go to bed. Do the same for your weekends. Also think in terms of what you do in a week or month.**

2. **Look through your list and take away the least important item.**

3. **Do this again.**

4. **Keep doing it until you get down to the top six.**

5. **Now, list the final six in order of importance.**

Below, you will find my personal example. The numbers beside the "strike-throughs" represent the order in which I struck them off. Sports, which I love dearly by the way, were first off the list and therefore has a "1" beside it. Successful speaking and consulting was the last to go and therefore had a "9" beside it. I discovered that "Fulfilling my purpose" was more important than how I actually did it.

15 Most Important Things

Optimum health	
Friends	6
Recreation	5
Loving relationship with my wife	
Successful speaking and consulting	9
Happy healthy children	
Sales calls	4
Financial freedom for my family	
Living a Godly life	
Sports	1
Church	8
Social events with friends	3
Helping my community	7
Sense of purpose	
Physical closeness	2

Greg's Top Six:

1. **Living a Godly Life**
2. **Loving relationship with my wife**
3. **Optimum Health**
4. **Happy healthy children**
5. **Sense of purpose**
6. **Financial Freedom**

If done seriously, this is a confronting yet freeing exercise. You may discover that the new car was not in the top five but your family was, yet you had been more focused on the car. You may also have re-discovered that your golf game was less important than your husband was. As well, you may realize that you've been spending more time watching TV than investing time with your children. Don't get me wrong—if you can do all the things on your list, then terrific, but the question to always ask is, "Am I taking care of my priorities first?"

If you want to make good use of your time, you've got to know what's most important and then give it all you've got.

—LEE IACOCCA

Stress is caused when you have your priorities out of "sync." Each year, each month, each week, each day, and each hour, you must ask yourself, **"What is the most important thing I can be doing at this moment in time?"** Be driven by your long-term goals. When you're excited about your goals and the life which they promise to bring about, you will do everything to maximise your time today in order to enjoy those achievements.

Make a to-do list and prioritise. Use the A-B-C method to prioritise. "A" means that it is both urgent and important. "B" means that it is important but not urgent, and "C" is everything else on your list. Too many of us get caught doing all the minor things when it's the major items that count.

Give up short-term pleasure for long-term gain. How often do we face a choice of fun versus duty, and naturally pick the former? How many times do we find ourselves procrastinating on an important task while engaging in a more pleasurable activity? When we learn to give up short-term pleasures, the subsequent progress and sense of accomplishment will fuel a fire within us to complete the project at hand.

Take care of the minutes. In my seminars, I ask people if they want to have a great life. The answer is always affirmative. The ways to achieve a great life vary depending on individual views. My answer is, "If you want to have a great life, have a great year – every year!" Needless to say, it causes eyes to roll. Then I ask another question, "How do you have a great year?" They ponder for a moment and someone in an interrogative tone says, "Have 365 great days?" And on it goes… How do you have a great day? Have 24 great hours. How do you have a great hour? Have sixty great minutes and then, of course, we hear the expression, "Make every second count."

If we take care of the minutes, the years will take care of themselves.

—BENJAMIN FRANKLIN

Get organised everywhere. There is no doubt that when you are organised, you feel less tense. When you know where things are, you avoid wasting time looking for them. Organise your closet, drawers, file cabinets, kitchen cupboards, basement storage area, car glove box, car trunk, computer files, etc. Can you see how many places in our lives we accumulate clutter? Don't be the pack rat. If you don't use it, lose it. Give it away and let someone else benefit from it, sell it, or trade it.

Piggyback by knowing your goals. When your goals are clear, you can piggyback on time and travel by combining tasks. For example, if you are going to be in a particular part of the city, you might arrange an appointment with your accountant who works in the area, arrange to drop off a package on the way there, or make a purchase at a store in the vicinity. By knowing your goals and plans, you save time and money.

Avoid task jumping—finish it now. You're working on something and the phone rings. This leads to something else, which leads to something else. Instead, when the phone rings say, "I'm in the middle of something, can we pick a time to speak later?" Or when you are interrupted by your own thoughts, write them down on your "to do" list and take care of it later. Studies show that it takes 60% longer to complete a task when you allow interruptions. If you can do it now, don't put it off until tomorrow. Take advantage of the opportunity. Keep saying in your mind, "*I do it now!*" Then do it!

Leverage yourself or delegate. Whenever possible, get someone else to do it. They may prefer it or they may be going that way or quite simply you shouldn't be doing it because it is a poor use of your time. If you feel it will take longer to show the person how to do the task, remember that over the course of a year you could save significantly more time than it takes to show them the ropes. If you're afraid it won't be done right, train them how to do it right. Support them until they get it right. Lastly, if you feel badly about giving the task to someone else, explain to him or her how important it is that you delegate it to them and ask for their understanding.

Trade things to do. Because we all have different talents and abilities, it may take someone less time than you to carry out a certain task. I'm sure there is something you can do with less effort and in less time than someone else can. Feel free to trade. Your partner may hate washing the car and you may hate ironing. However, he may enjoy ironing and you might enjoy washing the car. Work at discovering likes and dislikes and then trade chores and things to do. Your life will become more fun and efficient. It will also strengthen your partnership. You can practice the same thing at your workplace or personal life.

Try the Swiss cheese method. If you have a variety of projects running simultaneously, take a small action in each of them. It will give you a feeling of progression and momentum. It's called "Swiss Cheese" method because you're "punching holes" in the projects to get them rolling.

Plan time in 15-minute intervals. What is better, eight one-hour slots or 32 fifteen-minute slots? I know that you have calculated both to be eight hours of time but the point is that when you consciously think in fifteen minute time segments, it causes you to be more aware of time. It's the fifteen-minute losses here and there that add up over the course of a day. Three fifteen-minute slots for lunch can turn into five slots quite easily. Or, to make an appointment for two fifteen-minutes slots will keep you more focused than a half of an hour.

Avoid office and phone "slurpers." Have you ever noticed that when people have nothing to do they want to do it with you? When fellow team members come into your office to chat about golf or the weather, don't spend more than thirty seconds with them lest they "slurp" your time. Getting slurped is messy and noticeable at day's end when you realize that little was accomplished. When you are called on the phone, after a brief greeting say, "What can I do for you today?" or "How can I be of help to you today?" It politely lets people know that you mean business. And if there are times when you need to get out of a call, here are a few starters: "I really appreciate the call", or "Thanks for letting me know", or "May I pass you on to my assistant to take those details?" It is important for you to get them off the phone.

Avoid bringing work home. When you bring work home, you run the risk of becoming burnt out and resentful. The reason you are home is to be with family or to recreate. Instead, you're thinking about the work on your home desk (which doesn't get done half the time anyway). It is better to stay an hour later at work and then go home and spend quality time with family. An added benefit to staying later is that you spend less time in traffic. Another great strategy is to go in early and leave early.

The "race block time" method. When I have a task I dislike doing, instead of procrastinating, I challenge myself and say, "I'm going to get this paperwork completed in twenty minutes. Ready, set, go." Then I race against time. Before I know it, the task is done, and I actually had fun doing it. Try it with any of your drudgery tasks like paperwork, cleaning, and phone calls.

Have standard checklists. Keep checklists for activities that require detailed preparation, such as packing for business trips, vacations, camping trips, etc. Once the list is made, there's no more stress of having to remember all the details or going back home to get what you forgot.

Go to bed and get up a half-hour earlier. Early mornings are an excellent time to plan, visualise, read, meditate, and do your workout—all those things that you never seem to get done but are important. My friends sometimes chuckle at me when I go to bed between 9 or 10 P.M.. I arise at 5:30 A.M. and I can tell that I get a more done by noon than many people get done in a day…and it includes a workout and reading education. If you're thinking you could NEVER do that, please know that I use to think the exact same thing. When you try it and experience the benefits, you will surely continue doing it.

Turn off the television. If you reduce the time spent watching television by only thirty minutes per day, that's 182 hours a year, or 23 eight-hour days. Television can be an awesome educational and entertainment tool; however, in most cases we all could invest that time into something more beneficial. As a former teacher, I often heard students admit that television and computer games prevented them from doing homework at night. When their homework was not completed the night before, they would have the intent of doing it the next morning, which would then get transferred into noon hour; eventually it would not be completed at all. This would lead to poor results and plummeting self-esteem. The situation applies to adults who complain that they don't have time to exercise, do essential chores, spend quality time with the children, start the new hobby, write the book, or learn to invest. The solution to this is very simple - think of what you could accomplish with an extra 23 days in a year.

Hold meetings the right way. Many of us have sat in a meeting thinking about all the work we could have been doing instead. An efficient meeting should have an agenda, an action plan from the last meeting with names and completion dates and a start and finish time. If you're there on time, ask that the meeting start on time. If the meeting goes beyond its end time, quietly excuse yourself - your time is precious, and you are a good manager of it. Besides, you have your next fifteen-minute slot booked, right?

Accept what was completed. Be happy and accept what got done. If you wasted some time, learn from it. If you had a rough day, leave it behind. Count your victories only.

By maximizing your time each day you will be richer in wisdom and in reward. You will be controlling a key resource that has been given to you.

Chapter 16 — Summary

Have the Time of Your Life

- Take care of the big rocks first.
- Establish your top priorities.
- Be driven by long-term goals.
- Make a to-do list and prioritise A-B-C.
- Give up short-term pleasure for long-term gain.
- Get organised. - Clean up the clutter.
- Piggyback on goals.
- Avoid task jumping.
- Practice the "do it now" habit.
- Leverage or delegate.
- Trade things to do.
- Use the Swiss cheese method.
- Plan in 15-minute intervals.
- Avoid office and phone slurpers.
- Avoid bringing work home.
- Go to bed and get up a half-hour earlier.
- Turn off the TV.
- Hold meetings the right way.
- Accept what was completed.

Stay Fired Up!

17

BE WEALTHY BY BEING WISE

One of the weaknesses of our age is our apparent inability to distinguish our needs from our greeds.

—DAN ROBINSON

I must confess that I have made many mistakes in the realm of finances. I have lost on risky investments, made poor business decisions and spent money frivolously. In this rich society we can all be reasonably prosperous with a little hard work and intelligent money management. However, the cost of poor money management is high. When you are broke, it can affect your self-esteem, which in turn can affect the direction of your life. Don't let it happen. If you are in a tough financial spot, you simply must get out of it and get back on track. Pour your energy into it and know that you *can* succeed. The following wisdom comes from analysis of some of my mistakes as well as from credible sources representing those who have prospered financially. Follow these ideas and you *will* be successful and happy with your finances.

What Having Money Can Do For You

One of the most powerful stories in my life, which demonstrated the purpose for money, occurred when an old friend of mine was in trouble. I had lost touch with her after high school and twenty years later I found her in the city I was living in. She had just finished two years of a very expensive school program and was quite broke financially. When I questioned her about her food stores, the picture did not sound good. Right after the call I went grocery shopping and showed up at her door at 11pm. She was overjoyed and even cried at the sight of all the sustenance. I told her to cut out all that emotional stuff and let's eat. She unwrapped the groceries like Christmas morning had arrived and was unabashedly happy. Guess who was even more jubilant? I felt such a sense of joy that I had the financial means to help a fellow human being in trouble. You see, I had been in her shoes three years earlier and here I was helping her. This is one of the great reasons for financial prosperity. The more you earn, the more you can help your fellow human beings. That's way more satisfying for me than a new BMW…and I love BMWs.

Money can also buy a certain amount of security. If your home is paid for, you need not worry about it. If you know your investments will bring an income stream for retirement, you can look forward to enjoying that retirement. If you insure your car, home and life, you can rest assured that your family will be taken care of. Money can also bring you additional opportunities like a more comfortable home to enjoy, a more reliable car, the ability to travel and see this beautiful world of ours, upgrades to your education, and the list goes on. We must however, be cautious about money, for too much of it could also make us unhappy.

How Money Takes Away Happiness

It seems to me that when we view money as described above, it is good and can help to increase the quality of one's life and therefore happiness. If this is so, why are there so many unhappy millionaires, movie actors and people who have "made it" financially. Here are a few answers:

1. **They adopt values that don't line up with the definition of success.**
2. **They feel that money really will buy them happiness and continually get caught in the cycle of trying to earn more of it.**
3. **They allow the quest for money to overrun their principles and values for living.**
4. **They begin to see people as opportunities to make money versus opportunities to serve.**
5. **They justify their absence from family to earn more money to spend when spending more time with family would add more value and happiness.**
6. **They become "their status," that is, they think that wealth should be the reason people respect and admire them. They lose their humility.**

> *Before I had a lot of money, I was really quite happy. And, I will tell you this-you may not believe it-I never would have gotten the money if I wasn't happy to begin with.*
>
> **—OPRAH WINFREY**

The Benefits of Having Little Money

We don't have to be miserable during those times when we don't have a lot of money. We can use the time as an opportunity to learn, grow and be more creative. Here are some examples.

Time to educate
When I didn't have a lot of money, I had to find inexpensive ways to develop myself. I read more, volunteered more and spent more time developing my craft. While others were out having fun, I was developing myself.

Learn to be alone
Many people are hooked on having to be with people. They cannot bear to be alone. Part of being a successful human being is to learn to be alone in order to develop independence, to reflect, and to just be quiet.

Spend time with God or meditate on life
Our lives become so frenzied that we sometimes forget to be with our Creator. Like any good relationship, we need to spend time with God sharing our victories, our troubles and asking for His help. If you do not know God, perhaps you might use this time for reflection on the meaning of your existence.

It is possible that you may have excellent values and a good work ethic but you just can't seem to get ahead financially. Consider that you might have a poverty mentality. It can be linked to your self-esteem in that you may not feel worthy of having money or wealth. Remember that you have as much right to money as the next person but the key is you have to earn it. Why do so many immigrants come to Canada and the US with no money, education or language and yet they have thriving businesses after just a few years? Author and speaker Walter Hailey says that legal immigrants are four times more likely to become millionaires than people born in America. Why is this? It's because they have a high expectation or belief in the country and act in accordance with that belief. Before they get "pulled in" to seeing and believing all the negative things going on in the country, their belief and subsequent actions have caused them to be successful. Along with your positive attitude, by adopting the following concepts, you will dramatically increase your chances of becoming financially successful.

Build Your Character (Be-Do-Have)

The development of your character is the most important aspect of attracting money. My friend Dave Phillips reminds me that you have to "be" before you can "do" and when you "do" what you do well, you will "have." Work on becoming more disciplined, more knowledgeable, more aggressive, more confident, more polite, more educated and most of all more service oriented so that you are creating value as you are earning your money.

> *The character of the business owner is more important in predicting his level of wealth than the classification of his business.*
>
> **—THOMAS STANLEY, THE MILLIONAIRE NEXT DOOR**

Avoid get rich quick schemes

We live in a world that promotes get rich schemes, gambling, lotteries, and earning big bucks fast. Multi-level marketing is one of the fastest growing marketing ideas in the world and is an example of this kind of hype. Don't get me wrong. I think multi-level marketing is a wonderful idea that makes perfect sense. By cutting out main distribution systems and allowing the individual person to market and distribute, the consumer will save money both as a salesperson and as a buyer of the products. The problem is that the system promotes a get rich quick attitude. Meetings are often started by people getting up and announcing how much money they have made in a short period of time. There are copious other get rich schemes out there as well. Be careful. Fast money is the exception, not the rule. If you are going to engage the MLM or Network Marketing industry, I encourage you to read billionaire Peter Daniel's book on the subject. Then you can proceed with strategy and wisdom.

Overcome your poverty mentality

Get over the fact that you're poor and in debt. Accept it and take responsibility. Stop blaming others or the government. The government is not here to take care of you. God gave you an amazing brain and a wonderful body. If your body doesn't work that well then remember that there are *many* who work with their feet, or only one hand, or no vision and do quite well.

Create a vision for what you need and the kind of lifestyle you would like. If you keep dwelling on your awful situation, it will drag you down. Cut out pictures of what you would like to be and have - then take action!

Decide how you are going to contribute to the world. Decide how you're going to make this world a better place. A woman at Nassau Space Centre who was cleaning the floors was asked what she was doing. Her reply was, "I'm helping to put people into space!" You can be a gas station attendant or a CEO but be the best you can be. I stop at a station in Vancouver and they run out to serve me. I know that those employees will go on to do bigger and better things because of their great attitude.

Clear up your debt. Make agreements with your creditors and be honest with them. Running away will only make the problem worse. There are thousands of people who have been in debt and years later are doing quite well financially. Keep the vision and believe.

> *Buy the truth and do not sell it; get wisdom, discipline and understanding.*—The Bible

Educate yourself

I cannot stress enough the value of educating yourself by reading books, listening to tapes and associating with those who have found success by using sound economic principles. One book I recommend is called The Millionaire Next Door of which I will refer to in this chapter.

Avoid materialism

Many people criticise those who are wealthy for being materialistic. What is the definition of materialistic? Ask yourself how many times a day, week or month you think about money or what you don't have. Isn't *that* materialism? If you keep worrying about money, consider that you *are* materialistic. Stop worrying! Set your goals and get to work. Worrying will not add a single bit of cash to your net worth. Remember that money has never made a man happy yet, nor will it. There is nothing in its inherent nature to produce happiness. It is a means to an end.

> Better is little with the fear of the Lord, than great treasure, and trouble therewith. —Proverbs 15:16

Give money away or tithe

People are always being hounded to give money for this or that. There are so many wonderful organisations doing great things for the world and they all want and need your money. Decide what you want to give and whom you want to give it to and then give it with joy in your heart. Be glad that you have the privilege. I have adopted two children through the World Vision program. My $62 dollars a month (one evening out) does absolutely amazing things for those children, their families and their village. At another time I sent $262 to provide drug therapy to cure a person of leprosy. Think about that. I'm not blowing my own horn but telling you that you can do amazing things with very little money. $100 of your money is like $100,000 in some parts of the world. I love what John Wesley says about money:

> *Make all you can, save all you can, give all you can.*
>
> —JOHN WESLEY

If you don't have money to give, you can donate your time. You have a skill or labour to offer and this can be another way of giving back to the community.

Save and invest

If you can save ten percent of what you earn consistently all your life, you will likely be in an excellent position for retirement. If you are behind, there are ways to catch up but start today if you haven't already. The key to the ten percent rule is to have it taken from your paycheque automatically. If you have to rely on physically taking 10% from your paycheque and depositing it into your savings it is likely not going to happen. When you have it taken automatically, you forget that it was even there.

Be tax savvy

My current position on taxes is to pay them. However, many people lose out each year because they have poor knowledge about taxes. Either educate yourself or find a reliable accountant. As a business person, I save way more on taxes than I spend on my accountant. It may be that you are losing hundreds even thousands of dollars because of tax ignorance. I encourage every citizen to start their own business however small. Your overall tax burden will surely be reduced.

Avoid the lottery syndrome

Many people are living what I call the lottery syndrome. They honestly believe they're going to win the big one or an inheritance and therefore are not giving life their best effort. Despite what the amazing commercials on TV and radio are telling you, you're not going to win. Your chances are unbelievably poor and you have more chance of being hit by lightning. Again, you'll be happier about your money when you earn it.

Be honest

If you earn money dishonestly it will eventually catch up with you - maybe not today or tomorrow or even this decade, but it will cause you trouble in the end. Knowing that you are being dishonest will cause you to lose sleep, age prematurely, and affect everything you try to enjoy. You cannot escape dishonesty.

The authors of the book *The Millionaire Next Door* spent considerable time and money discovering how people became millionaires. Here are sixteen of what I felt to be the most important points within the book. I particularly liked how these millionaires have both excellent family and ethical values.

16 Millionaire Tips

1. They live well below their means.
2. They believe financial independence is more important than displaying social status.
3. They chose the right occupation.
4. Two thirds were self-employed.
5. Half of the wives do not work outside the home.
6. Most have been married to the same woman all their life.
7. 95% come from married households.
8. More than half invest first and then take care of their living expenses.
9. They have lifetime, annual, quarterly, weekly and daily goals.
10. They pay less tax on their taxable income.
11. 80% of millionaires in America are 1st generation.
12. They budget by category.
13. They spend time on financial planning.
14. They are not active investors. They tend to leave their money in investments and not move them around.
15. 77% drive a used vehicle.
16. A large majority love their work. They are excited when they wake up in the morning.

If you feel that your financial situation is desperate or that you are behind in your financial life, fear not. If you adopt these principles, over time (and this can mean 10 to 20 years) you *will* see your financial life change for the better. Again, desperate attempts to become rich seldom work. Do not fall into the trap of get rich quick schemes. Only by following sound principles will you become prosperous, both spiritually and economically.

Chapter 17 — Summary

Be Wealthy By Being Wise

- Learn to appreciate and use those times when you don't have money.
- Build your character first. It's who you "be" that will determine what you "have."
- Avoid get rich quick schemes.
- Decide that you will prosper.
- Give money away.
- Save and invest 10%.
- Avoid the lottery syndrome.
- Be honest.
- Have a plan and a budget.
- Live below your means.
- Love your work.

Stay Fired Up!

18

POWER UP YOUR ENVIRONMENT

You are free to choose but the choices you make today will determine what you will have, be, and do in the tomorrow of your life.

—ZIG ZIGLAR

Of all the ideas, tips, and techniques you have read about in this book, your environment can be the most important. You can be the most motivated person in the world, but if your workplace is constantly filled with negativity, eventually it will wear you down. Watch enough television and over a period of time, without realising it, you will become desensitised and more accepting of the status quo. Read enough questionable magazines and books and your mind will become polluted with silly ideas. Associate with enough negative friends, and you will become negative. Read enough newspapers and listen to sensationalistic newscasts and you will begin to lose hope for humanity.

Do not believe that you are making all your own decisions all the time. You may have been conditioned by the media or caught up in the frenzy of the latest car, fashion, movie, or moral value. The frightening part is that the shifting of values occurs slowly over time. It is a gradual and insidious transition. In the 1950s, a survey was conducted of the top ten problems in schools. The list included chewing gum, talking out loud, throwing paper and butting in line. The same survey conducted again in the 1980s revealed that drugs, alcohol, rape, sexual abuse, pregnancies, suicide, eating disorders, and school violence were the primary problems. There is no doubt that the culture of yesterday has influenced you today, and the culture of today is influencing your future right now.

Studies show that you become most like the five people with whom you spend the most time. Naturally, we should try to spend time with those who are going to build us up, encourage us, and who have a positive mental attitude. Should you now completely avoid all your negative friends? I don't think so, but you might consider spending less time with them. If they confront you about the reason, let them know why and try to bring them along with you on your journey. If you wanted to succeed in business, would you consider spending time with those who were failing, or those who were succeeding? If you wanted to be a good golfer, would you improve faster if you played with better golfers? Be aware that you may be keeping the company of those who keep you comfortable as opposed to those who are committed to your success. As a professional speaker, in pursuit of personal growth and improvement, I find it important to connect with those who are ahead of me in the game. I watch, listen, and emulate their strengths.

Boards of Advisors and Coaches

You should also strive to have your own board of advisors, or in the very least, your own coach. The world's best athletes have coaches because they know it's important to their success. Why don't *we* have coaches? You may be thinking that you don't want to be the best. Of course you do. You want to be the best father you can, don't you? You want to excel at your job and earn as much money as you can, don't you? You want to be happy, don't you? You want to be *your* best. Why not find people who can help you reach those goals? Allow others to contribute to your life by allowing them to coach you, either formally or informally.

Suppose you share my belief in having a mentor and learning from the best. However, you have doubts about being able to attract them. You might question why a highly successful person would spend time with you? I have discovered in my life that if you believe in yourself, others will want to get involved with you. Have a vision of how you would like to be, and act as if you have attained that level of success. Decide what you want in life and believe that you are worth being supported. Let a designated role model or coach know that you *will* be a success story, and they will be happy to guide you along your path to success. People enjoy being involved in the process of making someone a winner. Another way to attract winners is to serve *them* first. Look for ways to help them, whether it's sending a positive phone message or giving them a referral. Be open and sincere, be yourself, smile and let your joy shine through. People at all levels can't help but like that kind of a person.

Turn Your Car Into a University

If you listened to educational tapes, CDs, etc, on one subject for only 15 minutes per day and you did it 200 working days per year, that's 3,000 minutes, or 50 hours, of listening. That's like taking a half-credit college course. Get yourself some tapes on how to be a better parent, how to get along with your boss, how to be more passionate with your spouse, how to understand God, and so on. There are tapes on hundreds of subjects, recorded by experts who have achieved. If you travel by public transit, get a portable tape player.

Victory List

At the end of each day, tally up your victories, no matter how small they may be. The thoughts and feelings which you take to bed with you can have a strong bearing on the next day. Think about what went well during the day. Maybe you bought someone a coffee and gave an encouraging word. You might have landed a sale or at least got an appointment. Perhaps one of the children in your day-care spoke a word for the first time. You may have begun a new exercise routine and walked three blocks. Each day is *filled* with major and minor events that can be classified as victories. When you adopt this habit you begin to see the wonder of life. You will develop a more positive view and stand on the shoulders of your successes and not your failures.

The Morning Launch Sequence

Why not make the most of the circumstances you *do* have control over? You can get up in the morning thinking about the problems you have to face, the piles of work at the office, the irate customer from yesterday, or how angry your kids made you last night. You can turn on the radio and listen to all the bad news, or you can take control and make the mornings a great part of your day. I can testify that since adopting the habits below, I can't wait to go to bed earlier so I can get up earlier. I do most of the things on the list below and vary them from day to day:

- **Teach yourself to smile when you get up.**
- **Whether it's a nice day out or not, exuberantly say, "This is the first day of the rest of my life!"**
- **Read the Bible**
- **Read a motivational book.**
- **Read affirmations with enthusiasm.**
- **Drink a glass of purified water as soon as you get up.**
- **Go for a run around the block, even for five minutes.**
- **Take a hot shower and then turn it freezing cold.**
- **Eat a healthy breakfast and take vitamin supplements.**
- **Call or email someone and wish them a great day, or give them a motivational message.**
- **Give thanks to God that your heart is still beating.**

- **Review yesterday's victories.**
- **Write out your goals for the day.**
- **Give your spouse a big kiss.**
- **Put on your children's favourite music. (Blast it!) When they look at you in disbelief, give them a big hug and tell them you love them.**
- **Wave to someone you don't know in the traffic line up.**

On the days that I do these, I experience a higher quality of life. The key to deriving pleasure from the morning launch sequence is to do it even when you don't want to. Do it and the power of habit will take over.

Chapter 18 — Summary

Power Up Your Environment

- You become most like whom you spend time with. Spend time with winners.
- Get a board of advisors or a coach.
- Turn your car into a university.
- Reflect on your successes and do a victory list.
- Start your day positively.

Stay Fired Up!

You Are the Winner Be the Winner

Having read this book, you probably feel compelled to change your life for the better. I hope that you have been changing it throughout. Change *is* challenging but it is not to be feared. Change or transformation starts first with your *willingness* to change or see the world differently. The need for change arises out of a need to overcome pain or a desire to seek pleasure. (Remember that there is a strong correlation between pleasure and service to others.) It takes courage to put that change into action. There will be pain, maybe a lot of pain as you change, but the rewards for discovering and living by success principles far outweigh the pain of not changing.

Each day you have a magnificent opportunity to take life and make it a breathtaking adventure. While you may be burdened with some tough circumstances, you can take those circumstances and turn them into something remarkable. You can turn lemons to lemonade. You can take the irritations of life and turn them into pearls. You can take sadness and turn it into joy.

I hope you will agree that you can read this book over and over and still get value. While all the points are important for successful living, there are some that stand infinitely above the rest. I invite you to consider picking up for yourself an easy to understand copy (they do exist) of the world's best selling book (that's the Bible) and start reading at John 3:1. Keep reading until you get to the end of the book. It's really OK to ask questions, to be cynical even, but get answers to the question versus simply denying what you read. I do, however, predict that you *will* be amazed and filled with excitement!

Finally, I say to you: Face every adversity with boldness, courage and faith. You are one person who is unique in the world. God made you special. He designed you not as a whiner but as a winner. You *are* a winner, have no doubt. Think like one, speak like one and act like one and you will become the success you were meant to be.

Stay Fired Up For Life!

WARMLY,
GREG GERRIE

PROMISES

CHECK UP

I made same bold promises at the beginning of this book. The promises were conditional on *you* the reader. If you are unable to go down this list and answer "yes" to all of the objectives, fear not. Change takes time, sometimes a very long time. I have been working on mastering some of these principles for over a decade and I'm still working on them and expect to do so until the day I'm on my way to heaven. Keep reading and keep striving to achieve these. Go back and re-read the highlights. You will gain insights for years to come. Never make the mistake of saying you tried it and it didn't work. You've got to keep on trying it! I've left a few lines after each promise and you may wish to make your own comment on your progress or even a new commitment:

1. **Give you the kind of hope and encouragement that will help you to live life joyously.**

___

___

2. **Show you how to leave behind pain and regret and replace it with peace.**

___

___

3. **Teach you about the most important aspect of living which is seeking wisdom.**

___

___

4. **Share with you how to go after the right kind of success – success that brings lasting joy.**

5. Sell you on the fact that you are not stuck with your past, that you can develop new beliefs and attitudes to transform your life positively and forever.

6. Demonstrate the power of turning failures into successes.

7. Help you develop an exciting new vision for all areas of your life – show you how to dream the possible dream.

8. Show you how to live well and finish beautifully.

9. Teach you how to think and speak with power, passion and purpose and how that will change your mind and the mind of others.

10. Encourage you to foster high quality relationships that will enrich the lives of others as well as yours.

11. Persuade you how to take care of your billion dollar body and how that will affect the rest of your life.

12. Help you to maximize your time so you can have the time of your life.

____

____

13. Demonstrate how to surround yourself with people and environments that will propel you toward your goals.

____

____

14. Have you realize that the greatest gift of success to yourself will occur when you give the gift of yourself to others.

____

____

15. Help you see that you are a unique individual, that you've been a winner from the start and that you have a very special purpose.

____

____

Overall, what are the three greatest positive changes you have made or actions you have taken as a result of this book?

1. ____

____

2. ____

____

3. ____

____

TALK TO ME

...Please

Please drop me a letter or email and let me know if a positive impact has been made on your life. With your permission, we will post it on our website and maybe even in the next edition of this book. The more that others hear success stories of various kinds, the more they will be inspired in their motivation and actions.

When you contact me, would you also let me know:

1. **May I quote you?**
   yes ____ no _____.

2. **May I use your name after the quote?**
   yes ____ no _____.

   E.g. *Fired Up for Life was instrumental in helping me to make a new decision to find the job of my dreams.*

   MARY SMITH-SPUSM, COLORADO

3. **May I use your company name?**
   yes ____ no _____.

   E.g. *I used the goal setting formula that Greg talked about and now my whole team is "Fired Up for Life." Thanks Greg!*

   JOE PIRANI-MANAGER OF CUSTOMER SERVICE
   XYZ CORPORATION-TORONTO, CANADA

4. **Would you leave your phone number in case I need further clarification?**
   no ___ yes___ phone (_____) _______-____________

For contact information go to:

Gerrie Training Solutions International
www.greggerrie.com

BOOKS QUOTED

Bach, Richard. *Jonathan Livingston Seagull*

Canfield, Jack and Hansen, Mark Victor. *Chicken Soup for the Soul-Volumes I, II, and III.* Health Communications Inc.

Chopra, Deepak. *Ageless Body Timeless Mind*

Cooke, William H. *Success Motivation and the Scriptures.* Broadman Press

Danko, William and Stanley, Thomas. *The Millionaire Next Door.* Longstreet Press

Frankl, Victor. *Man's Search For Meaning.* Pocket Books

The Holy Bible, NIV

Hill, Napolean. *Think and Grow Rich*

Lewis, C.S. *The Four Loves*

Maltz, Maxwell M.D.. *Pyscho-Cybernetics.* Pocket Books

Martin, Francis P. *Hung by the Tongue.* (Phone1-318-988-0030)

Maxwell, John C.. *Developing the Leader Within You.* Thomas Nelson Publisher

McDowell, Josh. *Right From Wrong.* Word Publishing

Rogers, Carl. *On Becoming a Person.* Houghton Mifflin Company

Schultz, Howard. *Pour Your Heart Into It.* Starbucks

Swensen, Richard, M.D..*Margin-Restoring Emotional, Physical, Financial and Time Reserves to Overloaded Lives.* Navpress

Tracy, Brian. *The Psychology of Achievement* (tape series). Nightingale Conant

Ziglar, Zig. *Over the Top.* Thomas Nelson Publishers

GERRIE TRAINING

SOLUTIONS INTERNATIONAL
CUSTOM DESIGNED

Keynotes Speeches
Consulting Services
Seminars

Covering

- Leadership
- Team Building
- Thriving in Any Economy

Seminars & Keynotes Titles

The Power to Change	Dream the Possible Dream
Vision To Succeed	Thrive in Any Economy
Optimism in the Workplace	Leadership That Changes Lives

Fired Up Schools

As a former student and teacher Greg knows what goes on in the education system. He combines his knowledge of psychology and motivation with his passionate and compassionate personality to create programs that make a difference to students, parents, teachers, and the community.

Raising Self-Confident Children	Parents
Your Best Year Ever	Students
The Teacher Vitality Program	Teachers
Bridging the Gap	Parents/Teachers/Students

Getting to the Source of Right and Wrong

We will interview key people or a cross section of your people to determine the key challenges within your department or organisation. This process has proven very effective due to a process to determine hidden truths in a confidential manner. It will save your organisation time, frustration and money.

Favourite Organisations & Associates

Dave Phillips - Phillips Management Co.
Dave is a Former Olympic coach, National Ski team member and has broken two Guinness World Records for both Water and Snow ski duration. He also does workshops and keynotes on Life purpose, mission, vision, personal/business relationships and also serves as a life & business coach to clients around the world. **www.courage4U.com**

World Vision
Christian humanitarian organisation providing relief and development to countries in need. Child sponsorship for $31/month.

The Esteem Team
Olympic athletes in Canada speaking to children in schools about succeeding in life.

David C. Bentall - Family Business Expert
David is an advisor to family businesses, a commercial real-estate consultant, champion water-skier, gifted public speaker and personal coach. **www.nxtstep.net**

TESTIMONIALS

FROM LEADERSHIP PROGRAMS

He made me realize that there is hope.

NATIVE STUDENT-BRITISH COLUMBIA

Positively invaluable!

JANSON HOLLISTAR-TEACHER-VANCOUVER CANADA

Greg's work brings hope to the confusion.

MARY BRESLIN-PACIFIC ASSOCIATE STORES

Greg's athletic background and training combined with his life experiences and vibrant personality were an ideal combination to motivate my team.

KEITH CHICQUEN

COACH-SR. GIRLS FIELD HOCKEY CHAMPIONS(BC)

One of the most useful programs I have attended in a long time.

LOUISE BAYLES-TEACHER-BRITISH COLUMBIA CANADA

Greg's ideas and inspiration leaves you saying, "Yes, I can do this!"

MANAGER-CANADIAN TIRE CORPORATION

My Education students were charged and changed by your positive words and your humour.

HEATHER MACKAY-FACULTY OF EDUCATION-

UNIVERSITY OF BRITISH COLUMBIA

GREGORY A. GERRIE

Greg Gerrie holds degrees in Economics and Education from Queen's University in Kingston, Canada. He is also educated in military leadership through the Canadian Armed Forces officer-training program.

He has held positions at the University of Toronto, The Open Learning Agency, Murata Erie Electronics, Meadowridge Private School, Arctec Engineering and TMI Training of Canada. Greg has also worked at the North Pole, has been a construction worker, and has taught tennis professionally. He is the former President of the National Society for Performance and Instruction-BC and the Canadian Association of Professional Speakers-BC, Canada.

As a professional speaker, trainer and process consultant, Greg helps organisations embrace change, develop vision and lead leaders. His empowering keynotes have helped thousands to overcome poverty of the spirit and renew their passion to succeed. Greg has assisted many corporations and schools to determine individual training plans and management intervention systems to help the workplace be both effective and exciting.

Greg is an avid skier, golfer, tennis player and private pilot. He is married to his beautiful wife Tina and have a princess daughter named Sarah.

BOOK

TESTIMONIALS

Read this book from cover to cover. It is a must for anyone wanting to feel hopeful, inspired and energized. Greg not only talks the talk, he walks the walk."

VALERIE CADE LEE-CERTIFIED SPEAKING PROFESSIONAL
PAST PRESIDENT-CANADIAN ASSOCIATION OF PROFESSIONAL SPEAKERS

After days of rain & grey days ..the sun shone as I drove to work over a bridge. I saw fresh snow on coastal mountains & realized I loved going to work. Now I see sunshine on the mountains EVERY day of the year. Greg's book taught me to see the positive even when (apparently) not visible!

NICK COLLINS, ESL INSTRUCTOR & DIVISIONAL CHAIRMAN, CAPILANO COLLEGE NORTH VANCOUVER, CANADA

I have learned (the hard way) that it's easy to get off track when attempting to discern which principles in popular motivational books are consistent with those in the Bible. Fired Up for Life cuts to the heart of this issue and offers strategies that are very practical and easy to apply. Greg Gerrie's transparency about his ups and downs, successes and failures are a tremendous encouragement and source of inspiration. Reading Fired Up for Life is a must for anyone committed to personal and spiritual growth.

ANNE THORNLEY-BROWN,
PROFESSIONAL ACTRESS (DOC, DEGRASSI JUNIOR HIGH,)

The key points that made the most impact on me are:

- *Being responsible for managing my thoughts - thinking positively*
- *Avoid negativity*
- *Our values are the foundation of our goals*
- *Happiness is closely tied to helping/serving others*
- *If others can do it so can I*
- *Life is a process & each day is an opportunity to start fresh*
- *Worry, fear & anxiety are the root of our failures & we have to overcome our way of thinking to go forward*

STEPHANIE BARTEL
TELUS TELECOMMUNICATIONS TOP SALES

Greg Gerrie's inspirational book is a personal coach, motivating us toward goals in practical ways, on our progress to maturity.

ELLEN EDWARDS
EXECUTIVE COORDINATOR, NETWERCC
EDUCATIONAL ASSOC. FOR CAREER
DEVELOPMENT PRACTITIONERS - BC

Fired Up for Life is a must-read for anyone who wants to increase the quality of life. Greg Gerrie becomes the "Ultimate Coach" as you read the well-researched ideas in his book. Chapter three alone, "Seek Wisdom First" is an enrichment worth more than dollars can measure.

MICHAEL BOLDUC
AUTHOR OF THE POWER OF MOTIVATION &
THE ANTHONY ROBBINS STORY

Just finished the book. It was a great motivation for me and more importantly, provided a method for effective goal setting. What I enjoyed the most were the practical applications you gave as examples on how to apply these principles. To be honest with you, I consider the book to be a blueprint on how to get more out of life.

GREG RIGGS
SENIOR TRADE COORDINATOR
TRADE EXCHANGE CANADA

I've read many similar books on staying motivated. In fact I use a process much like Greg's, and yet I learned so much from his candour. Everyone who is going through the humbling, sometimes downright depressing process of making their dreams come true, will be inspired to keep on. I needed to hear how tough another successful person had it on the road to his living his dreams. Some days, I wanted to quit too, but along came Greg's book just when I needed it. Thank you Greg for opening your heart to us dreamers and visionaries that are on the journey to living a life of richness and light.

A TEACHER

Both practical and inspirational, Greg has brought together the essence of the best motivational and success authors under one cover. Greg's transparency allows us to know the man behind the words and see our lives in his story. Fired Up for Life is recommended reading for all my clients.

LAURA NORTH
TRUE NORTH COACHING
WWW.TRUENORTHCOACHING.CA

I have had the privilege of knowing Greg's encouragement personally. Everyone deserves to be reminded to become their very best….which is what Greg does in person, and in his book. Great, uplifting, and easy reading.

DAVID C. BENTALL
NEXT STEP FAMILY BUSINESS CONSULTING

The chapter on FEAR and the one on TIME MANAGEMENT really helped me immensely. So much so, that I am going to use what I learned in those 2 chapters to train others on my team, as well as other associates, to be able to overcome their fears and learn how to effectively manage their time so that they can grow themselves and their businesses. The whole book was very motivating.

MARJ EHRESMAN,
CREATIVE MEMORIES CONSULTANT AND LEADER

Greg selflessly shares his life, lessons, insights and strategies to make a difference in people's lives. In an overwhelming world, his book lights the way for us to follow.

JONI MAR
CERTIFIED PROFESSIONAL CO-ACTIVE COACH
FORMER TV NEWS JOURNALIST, CBC TV

ENRICH THE LIVES

OF YOUR LOVED ONES,
FRIENDS, CLIENTS, AND COLLEAGUES.

***Ask about fundraisers for your non-profit or charitable group.**

Name: ____

Position: ____

Company: ____

Address: ____

City: ____

State/Prov: ________________ Postal/Zip: ________________

Phone:__________________ Fax: ________________

E-mail:____

_________ Invoice us! _________

We have enclosed Payment: Visa ____ MC ____ AMEX ____

Number ____

Name on card ____

Expiry Date ____ / ____ By phone ____ Date ____

Signature ________________________________

Date ____

Printed in Canada